ROYAL COURT

D1169306

The Royal Court Theatre presents

THE WITNESS

by Vivienne Franzmann

THE WITNESS was first performed at The Royal Court Jerwood Theatre Upstairs, Sloane Square, on Friday 1st June 2012.

THE WITNESS is part of the Royal Court's Jerwood New Playwrights programme, supported by the Jerwood Charitable Foundation.

Vivienne Franzmann's commission was supported by funds from the Olivier Foundation.

Principal Sponsor

THE WITNESS

by Vivienne Franzmann

(in order of appearance)
Joseph **Danny Webb**
Alex **Pippa Bennett-Warner**
Simon **David Ajala**

Director **Simon Godwin**
Designer **Lizzie Clachan**
Lighting Designer **Oliver Fenwick**
Sound Designer **Carolyn Downing**
Casting Director **Amy Ball**
Assistant Director **Rosy Banham**
Production Manager **Tariq Rifaat**
Stage Managers **Jenefer Tait & Ella May McDermott**
Stage Management Work Placement **Lex Kelly**
Costume Supervisors **Iona Kenrick & Claire Wardoper**
Voice Coach **Michaela Kennen**
Set Builders **Footprint Scenery Ltd**

The Royal Court and Stage Management wish to thank the following for their help with this production: The Donmar Warehouse, ETT, Waterstones, Omlet, India Jane, www.zoriah.com & www.zoriah.net, Colin Hardy, Chris Redgrave, Angela and Barry Kelly, City and Islington College, Directsalesmeuk, www.microdigita.co.uk, Thomas Penberthy at Photoshop Elements Magazine, Paul Grogan at N Photo Magazine, Phoebe Landa, www.plweddingphotography.com, Sophie & Harreld Masereka.

THE COMPANY

VIVIENNE FRANZMANN (Writer)

Vivienne was born in London and was a teacher for thirteen years. She is currently Pearson Playwright in Residence for the Royal Court and Writer in Residence for Clean Break. Her first play, Mogadishu was nominated for an Evening Standard and an Olivier award. The Witness is Vivienne's second play.

THEATRE INCLUDES: Mogadishu (Royal Exchange Manchester/Lyric Hammersmith/national tour).

RADIO INCLUDES: Mogadishu, Ink Deep.

TV INCLUDES: Coming Up.

AWARDS INCLUDE: 2008 Bruntwood Prize, 2010 George Devine Award, Pearson Playwright Bursary.

DAVID AJALA (Simon)

THEATRE INCLUDES: Ruined (Almeida); Nation, Death and the King's Horseman (National); Hamlet, Love's Labours Lost, A Midsummer Night's Dream (RSC); The Swing of Things (Stephen Joseph); How To Steal a Diamond (Traverse).

TELEVISION INCLUDES: Munroe, Misfits, Silent Witness, Doctor Who, Hamlet, Trexx and Flipside, The Bill, The Revenge Files of Alistair Fury, Dream Team, Coming Up.

FILM INCLUDES: Offender, Payback Season, One Day, Emulsion, Following Footsteps, The Dark Knight, Adulthood, Kidulthood.

ROSY BANHAM (Assistant Director)

THEATRE DIRECTION INCLUDES: October 15th (503); Charity Begins at Home (Waterloo East); Edges (Edinburgh Fringe).

ASSISTANT DIRECTION INCLUDES: A Kind of Alaska, Krapp's Last Tape, Coasting (Bristol Old Vic); The Comedy of Errors (Tobacco Factory).

PIPPA BENNETT-WARNER (Alex)

THEATRE INCLUDES: Richard II, King Lear (Donmar); The Swan, Caroline or Change (National); Ruined (Almeida); Crocodile (Riverside Studios/SKY TV); Victory (Theatre Royal Bath); The Lion King (West End).

TV INCLUDES: George Gently, Case Histories, Come Fly With Me, Lewis, Lenny Henry In Pieces, Holby City.

AWARDS INCLUDE: Carleton Hobbs Bursary.

LIZZIE CLACHAN (Designer)

FOR THE ROYAL COURT: Jumpy (& West End), Wastwater, Our Private Life, Aunt Dan and Lemon, The Girlfriend Experience (& Plymouth Drum); On Insomnia and Midnight (Festival Internacional Cervantino, Guanajuato & Centro Cultural Helénico, Mexico City); Woman and Scarecrow, Ladybird.

OTHER THEATRE/OPERA INCLUDES: Rings of Saturn (Schauspiel); Crave/Illusions (ATC); The Trial of Ubu, Tiger Country (Hampstead); A Woman Killed With Kindness (National); Happy Days (Crucible); Far Away (Bristol Old Vic); Bliss (Staatsoper, Hamburg); Treasure Island (West End); Shoot/Get Treasure/Repeat (Paines Plough); Contains Violence, Absolute Beginners (Lyric Hammersmith); Money, Tropicana (Shunt/National); Amato Saltone, Dance Bear Dance, The Ballad of Bobby François, The Tennis Show (Shunt); Soldier's Fortune (Young Vic); Bedtime Story & The End of the Beginning (Union Theatre/Young Vic); Julie, Gobbo (National Theatre of Scotland); Factory Girls (Arcola); Ether Frolics

(Shunt/Sound & Fury); I'll Be The Devil, Days of Significance, The American Pilot (RSC); All in the Timing (Peepolykus national tour); Moonstone (Royal Exchange Manchester).

Lizzie co-founded Shunt in 1998 and is an Artistic Director of the company.

CAROLYN DOWNING (Sound Designer)

FOR THE ROYAL COURT: Our Private Life, Oxford Street, Alaska.

OTHER THEATRE/OPERA INCLUDES: Love Song (Frantic Assembly); Beautiful Burnout (Frantic Assembly/National Theatre of Scotland); Double Feature (National); King John, The Gods Weep, The Winter's Tale, Pericles, Days of Significance (RSC); Lower Ninth, Dimetos, Absurdia (Donmar); Angels in America, Millennium Approaches, Perestroika (Headlong); Gambling (Soho); Lulu, The Kreutzer Sonata, Vanya, State Of Emergency, The Internationalist (Gate, Notting Hill); After Miss Julie, Ghosts, Dirty Butterfly (Young Vic); After Dido (ENO); The Water Engine (503/Young Vic); Belongings (Hampstead); Moonlight & Magnolias (Tricycle); Andersen's English, Flight Path (Out Of Joint); Topdog/Underdog (Crucible), A Whistle In The Dark, Moonshed (Royal Exchange Manchester); Blood Wedding (Almeida); Stallerhof (Southwark); After Miss Julie, Othello (Salisbury); Arsenic and Old Lace (Derby Playhouse); The Watery Part of the World (Sound And Fury); Gone To Earth (Shared Experience); Is That All There Is, Hysteria (Inspector Sands); Amerika, Krieg der Bilder (Staatstheater Mainz); All My Sons (Broadway); Tre Kroner - Gustav III (Royal Dramatic, Sweden); 3rd Ring Out (Metis Arts); No Way Out (Huis Clos).

OLIVER FENWICK (Lighting Designer)

FOR THE ROYAL COURT: Disconnect.

THEATRE/OPERA INCLUDES: After Miss Julie (Young Vic); The Madness of King George III (Theatre Royal Bath & West End); The Kitchen Sink, If There Is I Haven't Found it Yet, The Contingency Play (Bush); My City (Almeida); Saved (Lyric Hammersmith); Huis Clos (Donmar); The Begger's Opera (Regents Park); Realism, Mongrel Island (Soho); 'Tis Pity She's A Whore, Hay Fever, A Doll's House (West Yorkshire Playhouse); The Holy Rosenburgs, Happy Now?, My Fair Lady (National); The Winter's Tale (Guthrie Theatre); Much Ado About Nothing, Mary Stuart (Sweden); The Drunks, The Grain Store, Julius Caesar (RSC); A Number (Menier Chocolate Factory); The Picture (Salisbury); Hamlet, The Elephant Man, The Caretaker, The Comedy of Errors, Bird Calls, Iphigenia (Crucible); Ruined (Almeida); Ghosts, Kean, The Solid Gold Cadillac, The Secret Rapture (West End); The Line (Arcola); Timing (King's Head); Mary Poppins (UK tour); Private Lives, The Giant, Glass Eels, Comfort Me with Apples (Hampstead); Endgame (Liverpool Everyman); Sunshine Over Leith (Dundee Rep & tour); The Lady from the Sea, She Stoops to Conquer, On the Piste (Birmingham Rep); Restoration, Cinderella (Bristol Old Vic); Henry V, Mirandolina, A Conversation (Royal Exchange Manchester); Heartbreak House (Watford Palace); Jack and the Beanstalk (Barbican); A Model Girl (Greenwich); Noises Off, All My Sons, Dr Faustus (Liverpool Playhouse); Hedda Gabler, The Chairs (Gate, Notting Hill); Follies, Insignificance, Breaking the Code (Royal & Derngate); Tartuffe, The Gentleman from Olmedo, The Venetian Twins, Hobson's Choice, Dancing at Lughnasa, Love in a Maze (Watermill); Fields of Gold, Villette (Stephen Joseph); Hysteria, Children of a Lesser God (Salisbury); Three Sisters, Wild, Wild Women and The Daughter in Law (Orange Tree); Electra (Sweden); The Merry Widow (Opera North/Opera Australia); Samson et Delilah and Lohengrin, The Gentle Giant, The Trojan Trilogy, The Nose (Royal Opera House), The Threepenny Opera (Opera Group).

SIMON GODWIN (Director)

FOR THE ROYAL COURT: Goodbye To All That (Young Writers Festival 2012), The Acid Test, Pagans (International Playwrights Season 2011), Wanderlust, Hung Over: Ten Short Plays About The Election (Rough Cut), Black Beast Sadness (Off the Wall Season Reading), Hassan Lekliche (I Come From There Season Reading).

OTHER THEATRE INCLUDES: A Kind Of Alaska, Krapp's Last Tape, Faith Healer, Far Away (Bristol Old Vic); The Winter's Tale (Headlong/Nuffield Theatre/Schtanhaus/UK tour); All the Little Things We Crushed (Almeida); The Country (Tabard); The Seagull, Habeas Corpus, Relatively Speaking (Royal & Derngate); Quartermaine's Terms (Royal & Derngate/Salisbury Playhouse); Mister Heracles (West

Yorkshire Playhouse); Romeo & Juliet (Cambridge Arts Theatre); All's Well That Ends Well (Straydogs/UK tour); Eurydice (Straydogs/BAC/Trafalgar Studios).

OPERA INCLUDES: Inkle and Yarico (Straydogs).

Co-founder of Straydogs Theatre Company. Simon is currently an Associate Director of the Bristol Old Vic and the Royal Court.

DANNY WEBB (Joseph)

FOR THE ROYAL COURT: Chicken Soup With Barley, Piano Forte, Trade, Blue Bird, Search and Destroy, Serious Money (& Broadway), Carnival War a Go Hot.

OTHER THEATRE INCLUDES: 13, The Gardens of England, As I Lay Dying, Murderers (National); Blasted, Progress (Lyric Hammersmith); The Ditch (Hightide Festival); The Philanthropist (Donmar); The Green Man (Plymouth Drum/Bush); Richard III (Crucible/tour); Art, Popcorn, Death and the Maiden (West End); Goldhawk Road, The Nest, California Dog Fight (Bush); Dead Funny (Hampstead/West End); Back up the Hearse (Hampstead); The Pool of Bethesda (Orange Tree); Hamlet (Old Vic); Night Must Fall (Greenwich). Also seasons with Glasgow Citizen's Theatre and Liverpool Playhouse.

TELEVISION INCLUDES: Strikeback 3, Above Suspicion, Endeavour, Sherlock, Death In Paradise, Being Human, Tucker, Holby City, Midsomer Murders, Hustle, Landgirls, The Bill, Trinity, Britannia High, Casualty, Most Sincerely, New Tricks, Lark Rise to Candleford, Honest, Bloodlines, Miss Marple, The Bill, Rise and Fall of Rome, Doctor Who, Inspector Lynley Mysteries, Nostradamus, Totally Frank, Lewis, Heartbeat, A Touch of Frost, Silent Witness, Waking the Dead, My Family, Uncle Adolf, Murder in Suburbia, Dogma, Pepys, Life Begins, Murder Squad, Henry VIII, Cutting It, The Hound of the Baskervilles, Torch, Outside the Rules, Shackleton, Mccready and Daughter, Take Me, The Knock, Harbour Lights, Dalziel And Pascoe, Frenchman's Creek, Venus Hunters, The Jump, Out Of Hours, 2.4 Children, The Cleopatra Files, Disaster At The Mall, King Of Chaos, A Perfect State, True Tilda, Sharman, Murder Most Horrid, Mrs Hartley And The Growthcentre, Our Friends In The North, Cardiac Arrest, A Woman's Guide To Adultery, Comics, Head Hunters, Poirot, Tales Of Sherwood Forest, Intimate Contact.

FILM INCLUDES: The Arbor, The Story of F***, Visiting Hours, The Courageous Heart Of Irena Sendler, Valkyrie, The Harvester, The Aryan Couple, Stealing Lives, The Upside Of Anger, Family Business, Shiner, In The Name Of Love, Still Crazy, Love And Death On Long Island, True Blue, Alien III, Robin Hood, Henry V, Defence Of The Realm, The Kid And The Green Baize Vampire, The Year Of The Quiet Sun, The Unapproachable, No Exit.

JERWOOD CHARITABLE FOUNDATION

Jerwood New Playwrights is a longstanding partnership between the Jerwood Charitable Foundation and the Royal Court. Each year, Jerwood New Playwrights supports the production of three new works by emerging writers, all of whom are in the first 10 years of their career.

The Royal Court carefully identifies playwrights whose careers would benefit from the challenge and profile of being fully produced either in the Jerwood Downstairs or Jerwood Upstairs Theatres at the Royal Court.

The programme has produced a collection of challenging and outspoken works which explore a variety of new forms and voices and so far supporting the production of 72 new plays.

These plays include: Anya Reiss' SPUR OF THE MOMENT and THE ACID TEST, Penelope Skinner's THE VILLAGE BIKE, Rachel De-lahay's THE WESTBRIDGE, Joe Penhall's SOME VOICES, Mark Ravenhill's SHOPPING AND FUCKING (co-production with Out of Joint), Ayub Khan Din's EAST IS EAST (co-production with Tamasha), Martin McDonagh's THE BEAUTY QUEEN OF LEENANE (co-production with Druid Theatre Company), Conor McPherson's THE WEIR, Nick Grosso's REAL CLASSY AFFAIR, Sarah Kane's 4.48 PSYCHOSIS, Gary Mitchell's THE FORCE OF CHANGE, David Eldridge's UNDER THE BLUE SKY, David Harrower's PRESENCE, Simon Stephens' HERONS, Roy Williams' CLUBLAND, Leo Butler's REDUNDANT, Michael Wynne's THE PEOPLE ARE FRIENDLY, David Greig's OUTLYING ISLANDS, Zinnie Harris' NIGHTINGALE AND CHASE, Grae Cleugh's FUCKING GAMES, Rona Munro's IRON, Richard Bean's UNDER THE WHALEBACK, Ché Walker's FLESH WOUND, Roy Williams' FALLOUT, Mick Mahoney's FOOD CHAIN, Ayub Khan Din's NOTES ON FALLING LEAVES, Leo Butler's LUCKY DOG, Simon Stephens' COUNTRY MUSIC, Laura Wade's BREATHING CORPSES, Debbie Tucker Green's STONING MARY, David Eldridge's INCOMPLETE AND RANDOM ACTS OF KINDNESS, Gregory Burke's ON TOUR, Stella Feehily's O GO MY MAN, Simon Stephens' MOTORTOWN, Simon Farquhar's RAINBOW KISS, April de Angelis, Stella Feehily, Tanika Gupta, Chloe Moss and Laura Wade's CATCH, Mike Bartlett's MY CHILD, Polly Stenham's THAT FACE, Alexi Kaye Campbell's THE PRIDE, Fiona Evans' SCARBOROUGH, Levi David Addai's OXFORD STREET, Bola Agbaje's GONE TOO FAR!, Alia Bano's SHADES, Polly Stenham's TUSK TUSK, Tim Crouch's THE AUTHOR, Bola Agbaje's OFF THE ENDZ and DC Moore's THE EMPIRE.

So far in 2012, Jerwood New Playwrights has supported Nick Payne's CONSTELLATIONS.

The Jerwood Charitable Foundation is dedicated to imaginative and responsible revenue funding of the arts, supporting artists to develop and grow at important stages in their careers. They work with artists across art forms, from dance and theatre to literature, music and the visual arts. www.jerwoodcharitablefoundation.org.

THE ENGLISH STAGE COMPANY
AT THE ROYAL COURT THEATRE

'For me the theatre is really a religion or way of life. You must decide what you feel the world is about and what you want to say about it, so that everything in the theatre you work in is saying the same thing ... A theatre must have a recognisable attitude. It will have one, whether you like it or not.'

George Devine, first artistic director of the English Stage Company: notes for an unwritten book.

photo: Stephen Cummiskey

As Britain's leading national company dedicated to new work, the Royal Court Theatre produces new plays of the highest quality, working with writers from all backgrounds, and addressing the problems and possibilities of our time.

"The Royal Court has been at the centre of British cultural life for the past 50 years, an engine room for new writing and constantly transforming the theatrical culture." Stephen Daldry

Since its foundation in 1956, the Royal Court has presented premieres by almost every leading contemporary British playwright, from John Osborne's Look Back in Anger to Caryl Churchill's A Number and Tom Stoppard's Rock 'n' Roll. Just some of the other writers to have chosen the Royal Court to premiere their work include Edward Albee, John Arden, Richard Bean, Samuel Beckett, Edward Bond, Leo Butler, Jez Butterworth, Martin Crimp, Ariel Dorfman, Stella Feehily, Christopher Hampton, David Hare, Eugène Ionesco, Ann Jellicoe, Terry Johnson, Sarah Kane, David Mamet, Martin McDonagh, Conor McPherson, Joe Penhall, Lucy Prebble, Mark Ravenhill, Simon Stephens, Wole Soyinka, Polly Stenham, David Storey, Debbie Tucker Green, Arnold Wesker and Roy Williams.

"It is risky to miss a production there." Financial Times

In addition to its full-scale productions, the Royal Court also facilitates international work at a grass roots level, developing exchanges which bring young writers to Britain and sending British writers, actors and directors to work with artists around the world. The research and play development arm of the Royal Court Theatre, The Studio, finds the most exciting and diverse range of new voices in the UK. The Studio runs play-writing groups including the Young Writers Programme, Critical Mass for black, Asian and minority ethnic writers and the biennial Young Writers Festival. For further information, go to www.royalcourttheatre.com/playwriting/the-studio.

"Yes, the Royal Court is on a roll. Yes, Dominic Cooke has just the genius and kick that this venue needs... It's fist-bitingly exciting." Independent

ROYAL COURT SUPPORTERS

The Royal Court is able to offer its unique playwriting and audience development programmes because of significant and longstanding partnerships with the organisations that support it.

Coutts is the Principal Sponsor of the Royal Court. The Genesis Foundation supports the Royal Court's work with International Playwrights. Theatre Local is sponsored by Bloomberg. The Jerwood Charitable Foundation supports new plays by playwrights through the Jerwood New Playwrights series. The Andrew Lloyd Webber Foundation supports the Royal Court's Studio, which aims to seek out, nurture and support emerging playwrights. Over the past ten years the BBC has supported the Gerald Chapman Fund for directors.

The Harold Pinter Playwright's Award is given annually by his widow, Lady Antonia Fraser, to support a new commission at the Royal Court.

PUBLIC FUNDING
Arts Council England, London
British Council
European Commission Representation in the UK

CHARITABLE DONATIONS
American Friends of the Royal Court
Martin Bowley Charitable Trust
Gerald Chapman Fund
City Bridge Trust
Cowley Charitable Trust
The Dorset Foundation
The John Ellerman Foundation
The Eranda Foundation
Genesis Foundation
J Paul Getty Jnr Charitable Trust
The Golden Bottle Trust
The Haberdashers' Company
Paul Hamlyn Foundation
Jerwood Charitable Foundation
Marina Kleinwort Charitable Trust
The Leathersellers' Company
The Andrew Lloyd Webber Foundation
John Lyon's Charity
The Andrew W Mellon Foundation
The David & Elaine Potter Foundation
Rose Foundation
Royal Victoria Hall Foundation
The Dr Mortimer & Theresa Sackler Foundation
John Thaw Foundation
The Vandervell Foundation
The Garfield Weston Foundation

CORPORATE SUPPORTERS & SPONSORS
BBC
Bloomberg
Coutts
Ecosse Films
Kudos Film & Television
MAC
Moët & Chandon
Oakley Capital Limited
Smythson of Bond Street
White Light Ltd

BUSINESS ASSOCIATES, MEMBERS & BENEFACTORS
Auerbach & Steele Opticians
Bank of America Merrill Lynch
Hugo Boss
Lazard
Louis Vuitton
Oberon Books
Peter Jones
Savills
Vanity Fair

DEVELOPMENT ADVOCATES
John Ayton MBE
Elizabeth Bandeen
Kinvara Balfour
Anthony Burton CBE
Piers Butler
Sindy Caplan
Sarah Chappatte
Cas Donald (Vice Chair)
Celeste Fenichel
Emma Marsh (Chair)
William Russell
Deborah Shaw Marquardt (Vice Chair)
Sian Westerman
Nick Wheeler
Daniel Winterfeldt

Supported by
ARTS COUNCIL ENGLAND

APPLAUDING
THE EXCEPTIONAL.

Coutts is proud to sponsor the Royal Court Theatre

THE RIOT CLUB HITS THE WEST END
11 MAY - 4 AUGUST 2012

A PLAY BY
LAURA WADE

DUKE OF YORK'S THEATRE • ST. MARTIN'S LANE, LONDON WC2N 4GB
PHONE: 08448717623 • ROYAL COURT THEATRE BOX OFFICE: 02075655000
POSHTHEPLAY.COM

THE WITNESS

Vivienne Franzmann

Characters

JOSEPH
ALEX
SIMON

This text went to press before the end of rehearsals and so may differ slightly from the play as performed.

ACT ONE

Scene One

A living room. Hampstead.

JOSEPH *and* ALEX *look at each other.* ALEX*'s bags lie on the floor.*

JOSEPH. There's something different about you.

    Beat.

    Your skin's darker.

    Beat.

    You look different.

    Beat.

    Beautiful.

    Beat.

    You look like a beautiful young woman.

    Beat.

ALEX. You look like a fat old man.

    Pause. He smiles and opens his arms. She smiles and goes to him.

    What've you been eating, for God's sake?

JOSEPH. *Fromage.*

ALEX. *Fromage?*

JOSEPH. *Oui.*

ALEX. *Juste fromage?*

JOSEPH. I found this website. They deliver. Luxury Cheesiness for your Easiness.

ALEX. You've been getting cheese online?

JOSEPH. You can get fertilised duck eggs off the internet. Did you know that?

JOSEPH *goes to a box, takes out a joint and lights it.*

You incubate them. Jackie from number ten got five. When they hatch, the first thing the ducklings see, they adopt as their mother. Jackie's bichon frise was watching when hers hatched. They think a bichon frise is their mum. They sleep in his bed with him. Ducklings in bed with a dog. With a bichon frise. Extraordinary, isn't it?

Beat.

She got three Khaki Campbells and a Silver Bantam. She got a Welsh Harlequin as well, but it didn't hatch. It was a dud.

Beat.

She tried to get her money back, but –

ALEX. Why does Jackie have ducklings?

JOSEPH. To go with her chickens, Doris, Mabel and Maud.

ALEX. Why does Jackie have chickens?

JOSEPH. Urban farming. Trifling with poultry. Growing your own. All that shit.

Pause.

You can get sperm, you know.

Beat.

From the internet.

ALEX. Duck sperm?

JOSEPH. No, human sperm. Man sperm. For dykes or ugly women who can't get a fuck. It gets couriered on a motorbike to keep it all swimmy.

ALEX *tuts.*

Just think, broadband, some spunk and a Kawasaki creates a new life. That is some serious twenty-first-century evolution. Every single day, without fail, I think the internet is amazing. You could probably get duck sperm too if you rooted round a bit. Although I'm not sure a duck produces sperm. I guess it must do, although I've never even seen a duck's cock, have you? Do you want some food? Haven't got much in, but I do have a wide selection of luxury cheese.

ALEX. You knew I was coming –

JOSEPH. I can offer you Vintage Lincolnshire Poacher, Tetbury Truckle, Old Amsterdam –

ALEX. You're going to have a heart attack.

JOSEPH. On McKenzies Oatcakes with quince and rose-petal jelly –

ALEX. You have a classic heart-attack body shape.

JOSEPH. And I have a lovely bottle of Château Cantemerle.

ALEX. You store fat round your middle. It's indicating what's going on inside. All your organs are surrounded by fat, being suffocated probably.

JOSEPH. I've got some Crunchies if you want one.

ALEX. Your essential organs are being drowned by cheese and Crunchies.

Beat.

JOSEPH. Why don't we go out for dinner?

Beat.

Let's do that. We could go to that sushi place you like.

ALEX. Me Love Sushi.

JOSEPH. I know you do.

ALEX. That's what it's called.

JOSEPH. I know.

Beat.

ALEX. I'm tired, I think I'm just going to…

JOSEPH. It must feel a bit… You know… being back. You must –

ALEX. The train was so noisy.

JOSEPH. I thought you were going to reserve a seat in the quiet carriage.

ALEX. You're allowed to talk in the quiet carriage.

JOSEPH. Are you?

ALEX. You're allowed to talk as loud as you want.

JOSEPH. I thought –

ALEX. You're allowed to shout if you feel like it. You're allowed to sit in a group of middle-aged women and shout about Martin Amis all the way to King's Cross.

JOSEPH. Are you?

ALEX. Yes, if Martin Amis is your second cousin, apparently. But you can't speak on your phone.

JOSEPH. Could've been worse. They could've –

ALEX. When I got on the Tube, there was puke all over the seat. At first I thought someone had spilt one of those Innocent Smoothies, but then I smelt it –

JOSEPH. How revolting.

ALEX. So I moved and I sat next to this man who started singing Rihanna songs and asking me where I was from.

JOSEPH. Sounds like the journey from Jalalabad to Kabul.

ALEX. Whatever.

Pause.

JOSEPH. Why didn't you travel back with Lily?

ALEX. She's staying over the summer. She's got a job.

JOSEPH. That's a shame.

ALEX. I don't see that much of her anyway. She met this boy.

Pause.

JOSEPH. Shall I take your bag up to your room?

ALEX. I'll do it in a minute.

Pause.

JOSEPH *starts humming 'Umbrella' by Rihanna, and sings the first couple of lines from the chorus.*

Don't.

He sings another line.

Stop it.

He sings another line.

It's not becoming for a man of your age.

He continues to sing. He pulls her up.

Get off. I mean it.

JOSEPH. Don't you like it? What about this? (*Sings a few lines from 'Rude Boy' by Rihanna.*)

ALEX. How do you even know that?

JOSEPH. Got my finger on the pulse, got my –

ALEX. I'm going to unpack my stuff.

JOSEPH. What about food?

ALEX. I'll get a sandwich later.

She goes to go.

JOSEPH. I've got something for you.

He goes to a drawer and pulls out a small box.

(*Handing it to her.*) To celebrate.

ALEX. Celebrate what?

JOSEPH. Your first year.

ALEX. What about it?

JOSEPH. I'm proud of you.

ALEX. There's no need.

JOSEPH. I always knew that you could do it.

ALEX. I haven't done anything.

She opens it and takes out an antique necklace.

It's beautiful.

She puts it on. He helps her.

JOSEPH. We always planned to give it to you now.

ALEX. Thank you.

JOSEPH. At the end of your first year. It was Meg's grandmother's.

She rummages round in her bag. She pulls out a parcel and hands it to him.

What for?

ALEX. Because.

JOSEPH. Because what?

ALEX. Just because.

JOSEPH. Just because what?

ALEX. Because aside from the cheese thing, you seemed to have coped remarkably well.

JOSEPH. What is it?

ALEX. Open it.

JOSEPH. Give me a clue.

ALEX. Open it.

JOSEPH. It feels squidgy.

ALEX. Open it.

JOSEPH. Is it something to wear?

ALEX. Do you want me to do it?

JOSEPH. I could do with some new clothes. I've had this since –

ALEX. Give it here.

JOSEPH. I'm savouring it. Concentrating the mind on the present moment, as the Buddhists would have it.

ALEX. Just bloody open it.

JOSEPH *opens it. It's a hoody with 'King's College' on the front. He holds it up.*

JOSEPH. I love it.

He tries it on. She helps him.

ALEX. If I'd known about your saturated fat intake, I would've got an extra-large.

JOSEPH. It's perfect.

ALEX. It suits you.

JOSEPH. Thank you

He hugs her. Pause.

ALEX. Has everything been alright? Here on your own, has –

JOSEPH. Getting used to the utter lack of mess and filth everywhere has been terrifically hard, but –

ALEX. Dad…

JOSEPH. It's been fine. Everything's been fine.

ALEX. I knew it would be.

Beat.

JOSEPH. And what about you?

ALEX. Yep, good.

JOSEPH. Are you sure?

ALEX. Yes, I'm sure.

JOSEPH. Are you sure you're sure?

ALEX. Yes, I'm sure I'm sure.

JOSEPH. Yes, but are you sure that you're sure that…

ALEX.…sure that you're sure. Yes, Dad, I'm sure.

Scene Two

ALEX *is sitting on the sofa. She is reading a book, listening to her iPod. A muffled yell offstage.* ALEX*'s iPod runs out of juice. She takes it off and plugs it in to recharge. She reads her book. She takes a cushion and tries to put it over her head, balancing it while she reads. She is able to do this for a short time until it falls off. She gets up and puts on the radio; Radio 4 comes on. She retunes it to a pirate radio station. She turns it up. She lies on the sofa and attempts to read her book. The music is ridiculously loud.* JOSEPH *enters in his pants and turns the radio off.*

JOSEPH. What time is it?

ALEX. Nearly two.

JOSEPH. I said to wake me up at twelve-thirty.

ALEX. I forgot.

JOSEPH. You said you'd wake me.

ALEX. I was reading.

JOSEPH. I've missed *Loose Women*.

ALEX. Holy shit.

JOSEPH. And I'll be up all night now.

ALEX. Well, if you will have a nap in the middle of the day like an old man.

JOSEPH. I am an old man.

Beat.

Why aren't you at the interview?

ALEX. It's tomorrow.

JOSEPH. You said it was today.

ALEX. No. I said it was tomorrow.

JOSEPH. I'm sure you said –

ALEX. Tomorrow. Yes, I did.

Beat.

JOSEPH. I still don't know why you want to work there.

ALEX. Shut up about it, will you?

JOSEPH. I said I'd be happy to –

ALEX. I don't want you paying –

JOSEPH. It's only for the summer. It's only –

ALEX. Shut up.

JOSEPH. What the hell were you listening to anyway?

ALEX. Dunno. Some black station.

JOSEPH. There's headphones in there – (*Points to cabinet.*)
Use them.

ALEX. I was listening to my iPod, but –

JOSEPH. Use them.

ALEX. Yeah, alright.

He goes to the cabinet and gets them.

It's alright. I don't –

JOSEPH. I'll show you how.

ALEX. You don't need –

JOSEPH. For next time.

ALEX. I think I can work it out.

JOSEPH. This bit here goes in here. Can you see?

ALEX. Yes.

JOSEPH. Get up and look.

ALEX. I don't need to.

JOSEPH. Come over here.

She does. She looks at the stereo and the headphones.

See?

He hands her the headphones.

I stink.

ALEX. Yeah, you do.

JOSEPH. I need a shower.

ALEX. Don't let me stop you.

He goes to go out.

Don't take my shower puff.

JOSEPH. I wouldn't dream of it.

He walks out.

ALEX (*calling*). And don't you dare use my ginseng scrub.

He goes up the stairs.

(*Calling.*) I can hear if you walk into my bathroom. I'll hear you. I can hear from here. Don't even think about it.

She listens. He bangs across the floor above her. She tuts. She pushes her feet down the end of the sofa and wiggles them. She pulls out an old Crunchie wrapper with her feet. She pushes her feet down again, finds another. She reaches forward and pulls out five wrappers all stuffed down the end of the sofa. She winds the cord of the headphones up and puts them back in the cupboard. As she does so, she sees a photo album. She pulls it out and slowly starts looking at it. She puts the radio back on, retunes it to 6 Music and sits looking through the photos.

JOSEPH *enters in his dressing gown.*

That was quick.

JOSEPH. Washed my pits and had a shit instead.

ALEX. TMI.

JOSEPH. What?

ALEX. Too Much Information.

JOSEPH. Oh right. LOL.

ALEX (*pointing to photographs*). What are these?

JOSEPH. Photographs.

ALEX (*pointing at a picture*). Who are these people?

JOSEPH. Tom and Emily.

ALEX. Who are Tom and Emily?

JOSEPH (*pointing at picture*). That's Tom and that's Emily.

She looks at him.

ALEX. Why have you got this?

JOSEPH. I shot their wedding.

ALEX. You took these?

JOSEPH. That's what I said.

ALEX. Why?

JOSEPH. Because they were getting married and they wanted some photographs of it. I know, weird, isn't it?

Beat.

She's Claire's daughter.

ALEX. Who's Claire?

JOSEPH. I thought you knew Claire.

ALEX. No.

JOSEPH. She must have moved in after you left. She's at number eighteen.

Beat.

ALEX. And?

JOSEPH. And what?

ALEX. You're beginning to get on my nerves.

JOSEPH. I was speaking to her in the Post Office and she said that her daughter was getting married and they needed to find a photographer.

ALEX. So?

JOSEPH. So I volunteered.

ALEX. When?

JOSEPH. Last autumn. November, I think. That's why she's wearing that colour. I kept saying her dress was brown and she kept correcting me and saying it was 'rust' and that Amanda Wakeley had designed it to accent the amber in her eyes.

ALEX. Why didn't you say?

JOSEPH. I just thought it was a one-off, a favour. A favour for a neighbour. A neighbourly favour. It's nothing.

Beat.

ALEX. You should have told me.

JOSEPH. If I'd seen you, I would have.

ALEX. We spoke every week. I rang you every week. You should've told –

He goes to the cupboard and brings out three more albums.

JOSEPH. And then I did Steve and Amanda's in December, Kizzi and Sam's in January and John and Michael's in May.

He hands them to her. She looks at him.

Look at John and Michael's. Theirs was the best. It's true about the queers having great taste. It was at Kenwood and it was fantastic.

She looks at him. He ignores her and starts going through the book. She looks at him. Pause.

I like doing it. I like –

ALEX. Do they know who you are?

JOSEPH. Yep, Joseph from number thirty-four.

ALEX. You can be such a knobhead sometimes.

JOSEPH. Nice way to talk to your father.

The phone rings. She gets up. He looks through the photographs.

It'll be BT. They're always on at me, whinging about taking them back, like a bloody jilted lover –

ALEX. It's Paul. He phoned earlier.

JOSEPH. Leave it.

She answers it.

ALEX. Hello... Hi, Paul... Yeah, he's here... (*Laughs.*) yeah...
Yeah...

JOSEPH *tuts and takes the phone from her.*

JOSEPH. Hi... Yeah, fine, can we talk later? I was just in the
middle of something with Alex...

ALEX (*calls*). Don't mind me.

JOSEPH (*shut-up signs*). No, not really. No, I haven't. I need to
go. I'm on my way out... No, no, I haven't... I told you I
don't want to... No... I know... I know... Yeah, alright, I'll
call you... Yeah... next week some time... I said so, didn't
I? Yeah, sure... Cheers... Bye.

Pause. ALEX *studies the photos hard.*

ALEX. Where are you going?

JOSEPH. Nowhere.

ALEX. I thought you were going out. You told Paul you were –

JOSEPH. I am. I'm going to the shop.

ALEX (*indicating dressing gown*). In that?

JOSEPH. Yes.

ALEX. What are you buying?

JOSEPH. Five bottles of WKD and a family pack of Lambert
and Butler. What is this, Abu fucking Ghraib?

Pause. She looks at him.

He wants me to do an exhibition.

ALEX. Does he?

JOSEPH. I don't –

ALEX. Of what?

JOSEPH. Everything.

ALEX. Everything? Like a retrospective?

JOSEPH. Suppose so.

ALEX. Bloody hell.

JOSEPH. Yeah.

ALEX. Where?

JOSEPH. Starting in London.

ALEX. Where?

JOSEPH. The Imperial War Museum. There's talk of the V&A and –

ALEX. Bloody hell.

JOSEPH. And then touring.

ALEX. Bloody hell. How many images do they want?

JOSEPH. I don't know.

ALEX. I suppose it's all digital now. Do you have to get them transferred over or something?

JOSEPH. No idea.

ALEX. I bet it's quite easy. I guess Paul can arrange all that. God, there must be thousands, tens of thousands. How will you choose? Mum always said the stuff in Cambodia was –

JOSEPH. I'm not doing it.

ALEX. What?

JOSEPH. I don't have time.

ALEX. Yes, you do.

JOSEPH. I don't. I'm too busy. I'm –

ALEX. Too busy watching *Loose Women* and going to gay weddings?

Pause.

There's this artist, in Cambridge, Helen Someoneorother, she had this show and she used that picture of that stoning in Iran, you know the one of the woman buried in the hole, like that Beckett play, she took that and turned it into a collage of a heron.

JOSEPH. Sounds interesting.

ALEX. Shit. It was shit.

JOSEPH. Well, yeah, does sound shit actually.

ALEX. And the reviewer referenced you. He said he'd rather have spent the hour looking at one of your shots than her whole show. Or something like that. He said –

JOSEPH. That's the first thing you've told me about Cambridge.

ALEX. Yeah, but –

JOSEPH. I've been waiting for you to tell me.

ALEX. There's nothing to tell. You should –

JOSEPH. I want to know about your life there.

ALEX. There's nothing to know.

JOSEPH. What about your course?

ALEX. What about it?

JOSEPH. What's it like?

ALEX. Okay. Good, I suppose.

JOSEPH. And what about your boyfriend?

ALEX. What boyfriend?

JOSEPH. I thought you might have a boyfriend.

ALEX. No.

JOSEPH. You've had boyfriends before. There was Luke and then Harry and that one with ludicrous hair and the girl's name –

ALEX. I don't have time.

JOSEPH. Why not? What do you do?

ALEX. I go to lectures. I go to the library. I work in the bar.

JOSEPH. You must have made some new friends.

ALEX. Not really.

JOSEPH. But you must –

ALEX. I don't care about friends.

Pause.

You have to do this, Dad.

Beat.

People should see all your work, not just the famous stuff. If it all just sits boxed up in the cellar, what's the point of it? You may as well get rid of it. If no one sees it, what's it for?

JOSEPH. I don't want to.

ALEX. But –

JOSEPH. Alex, I said no.

Scene Three

JOSEPH *sits on the sofa.* ALEX *returns from work. She walks in wearing a Sainsbury's uniform, holding an almond tart.*

ALEX (*starts taking off her coat*). Got this for pudding. I couldn't remember if you love almonds or if you hate them. Mum loved them, but I couldn't remember about you. I know it's one or the other but it was only 50p because it's out of date so not much of a gamble. I thought I could eat my half and if you didn't want yours we could chuck it in the garden for the fox. Because I don't want the whole thing and it's too tempting if it's lying around. I can't stop myself, I'm such a bloater, I can't –

JOSEPH. I bumped into Lily today.

Beat.

She's working in the Tate Modern shop.

Beat.

For the summer.

Beat.

She asked about you.

Beat.

She said that you ignore her texts and emails.

ALEX. I don't like her. She's –

JOSEPH. She said that she hasn't seen you since last November.

Beat.

She said that she hasn't seen you since you left King's.

Beat.

Last November. She said she doesn't know why you dropped out. She said in November, you told her you were leaving. She tried to persuade you to stay, but you said your mind was made up and that you'd already told your tutors. She said you moved out of halls and she hasn't seen you since. She said she was worried about you, that she wanted to call me and ask me if there was something wrong, but she didn't know if that was the right thing to do. She said she missed you. Lily had an awful lot to say about you, Alex. She said she was surprised I didn't know. Not as fucking surprised as me, I said.

ALEX. I need to get changed.

JOSEPH. What happened?

Beat.

What happened at King's?

ALEX. Nothing.

JOSEPH. It must have.

ALEX. It didn't.

JOSEPH. You dropped out over six months ago.

ALEX. I didn't like it.

JOSEPH. Why?

ALEX. I just didn't.

Beat.

JOSEPH. What have you been doing?

ALEX. Nothing.

JOSEPH. Where've you been living?

ALEX. A studio thing. They call it that. It's a bedsit really.

JOSEPH. Where?

ALEX. In Cambridge.

JOSEPH. What have you been doing?

ALEX. Working in a bar.

Pause.

JOSEPH. Why didn't you talk to me?

Beat.

Why didn't you come home?

Beat.

ALEX. I couldn't.

JOSEPH. I wouldn't have been angry with you. I would've understood. We could have talked –

ALEX. It's not that.

JOSEPH. What then?

ALEX. I just felt…

JOSEPH. Yeah?

ALEX. I don't know.

JOSEPH. Was it the people? The other students? Were they…

ALEX. No.

JOSEPH. What about the people in halls? I thought you liked some of them. What about the girl that lived next door to you? What was she called?

ALEX. Jen.

JOSEPH. You got on well with her, didn't you?

ALEX. Yeah, she was okay, she was nice, she was fine.

JOSEPH. I don't understand.

Pause.

Please.

Beat.

Alex.

Beat.

ALEX. There was this boy –

JOSEPH. I knew it. I knew it would be about a bloody boy.

ALEX. It's not like that. It wasn't –

JOSEPH. Who is the little bastard?

ALEX. Just listen, will you?

Beat.

I was in the bar one night and this boy came over and started talking to me.

JOSEPH. Fucking little pervert. Did he spike your drink? Did he –

ALEX. At first it was just the normal stuff about our courses and where we were from, you know, small talk, nothing really. But then he asked me how I washed my hair and I thought he was weird and when I was thinking about what I could say to get rid of him, he reached over and he put his hand on my head.

JOSEPH. Yeah?

ALEX. He touched my hair.

JOSEPH. So?

ALEX. He leant over, like this – (*Leans over and fingers the texture of his hair.*)

JOSEPH. Maybe he liked you. Maybe it was a clumsy attempt to –

ALEX. He said I was the first black girl he'd ever spoken to.

JOSEPH. And?

ALEX. How can someone reach eighteen and never have spoken to a black girl?

JOSEPH. He probably went to some little prep school in Wiltshire, then Marlborough and on to a crammer where he was too scared to talk to any girls, never mind black girls. Is that why you left? Are you seriously saying –

ALEX. It wasn't right for me.

JOSEPH. We talked about this before you went.

ALEX. I didn't feel right there.

JOSEPH. About what to expect.

ALEX. I know, but –

JOSEPH. You can't tell me that you're the only black girl at
King's. You can't tell me that some skinny white virgin with
a hair fetish made you leave. I know you, Alex. I know you,
so stop bullshitting me and tell me the truth.

Beat.

 Is it drugs?

ALEX. No.

JOSEPH. Were you pregnant?

ALEX. No, course not.

JOSEPH. Did someone hurt you?

ALEX. No.

JOSEPH. What then? You'll need to help me out here, because
I've seen a lot of shit and I've got all sorts flying round my
brain. What happened?

Beat.

ALEX. I can't tell you.

JOSEPH. It can't be as bad as I'm imagining.

ALEX. I can't.

JOSEPH. Just tell me.

ALEX. I –

JOSEPH. Just fucking tell me. Fuck. For fuck's sake, Alex.

Pause.

Sorry. Sorry.

Pause.

ALEX. Lily's right, I did like it. For the first time since… in
ages… I felt…

Beat.

I made some nice friends and it was all going really well and
then that boy in the bar, he…

JOSEPH. Yes?

ALEX. He touched my hair.

Beat.

JOSEPH. And what else? What else did he do to you?

ALEX. Nothing.

JOSEPH. What are you talking about?

Pause.

ALEX. I didn't like it.

JOSEPH. What the fuck are you going on about? I think you've
gone completely fucking mad. What –

ALEX. I had this lecture on religious iconography –

JOSEPH. What?

ALEX. The next day, I had this lecture and Dr Kalmar put up a
slide of Botticceli's *Madonna and Child* and he made some
connection with contemporary photojournalism and when he
put up the next slide, it was yours.

Beat.

One minute, I'm trying to find my mobile, because Dr Kalmar
goes ballistic if anyone's phone rings and I'm cursing having
such a big bloody bag and laughing with this boy Stuart and
the next, I look up and there it is, filling the whole wall.

JOSEPH. Which one?

She looks at him. He knows.

Alex, I'm –

ALEX. And I feel like I'm going to faint or puke. And the
whole time Dr Kalmar's talking, I'm worrying in case I do
because it would be so embarrassing. And I'm trying to work
out which would be more embarrassing, puking or fainting,
and I'm trying not to look at the photo, but trying to look as

if I am and trying not to look like I'm about to faint and puke
and then Dr Kalmar stops talking. It's all quiet apart from
this noise at the back of the lecture theatre. Someone's
crying. And it gets louder and louder and I look round and
it's this girl from Surrey who's in my seminar group and
she's crying. And by now the girl is hysterical and one of her
friends is helping her out of the hall. And I stand up to leave,
but I go all dizzy and fall onto Stuart. Then Dr Kalmar looks
at me, turns the projector off, makes a joke about mass
hysteria and cancels the lecture.

JOSEPH. That must have been really –

ALEX. Afterwards, I'd arranged to meet Jen and I see the girl,
the crying girl, in the bar and I go up and see if she's okay,
because I feel bad for her, you know, responsible. I know it's
stupid, but... And when I ask her if she feels better, she says
she's fine, that she's having a bad day, that she's split up with
her boyfriend and is gutted because she loves him. She says
the photo made her feel awful, stirred something up and she
says she's embarrassed, but laughs and says it was cathartic.
Cathartic. That's what she says.

Beat.

She was crying because she'd split up with her boyfriend.
She looked at that photo and it made her think of what she'd
lost. In that photo, I'm screaming for my dead mother on a
pile of bloody corpses and that bitch is crying about her
fucking boyfriend.

Pause.

In that moment, Dad, in that bar, everything I thought I
understood about the world, and my place in it, turned to shit
and that's how it's been ever since.

Pause.

I want you to do the exhibition.

JOSEPH. Alex, this isn't about my work –

ALEX. I want you to.

JOSEPH. Or even that photograph –

ALEX. You have to.

JOSEPH. Or some white boy touching your hair or –

ALEX. Please.

JOSEPH. All the stuff with Meg's illness and all your hard work to get to King's, something was bound to give. It's a blip, darling, it's –

ALEX. I need to know that it matters.

JOSEPH. It won't make any difference to how you feel.

ALEX. I need proof that your work matters.

JOSEPH. It won't make any difference.

ALEX. Are you saying you won't?

JOSEPH. I'm saying it's not the answer.

Scene Four

ALEX *is on the laptop and on the phone in the living room.*
JOSEPH *is reading* Grazia.

ALEX. Yeah, a flight to Kigali… Kigali in Rwanda… You do, because I'm looking at it on your website. Yeah. Kigali. K–I–G–A–L–I. Yep… (*To* JOSEPH.) They don't even know where it is… (*Back on phone.*) Just one… From mid-October… I don't know. Two weeks… Maybe longer.

JOSEPH *looks up.*

How much?… But it said four-twenty on the website… That's false advertising… That's outrageous… I'm going to report you to Ofcom.

JOSEPH (*not looking up*). The Advertising Standards Authority.

ALEX. I'm going to report you to the Advertising Standards Authority… You can't just… It's illegal… What?… You can't say that… No, you go fuck yourself. (*Puts the phone down.*) Bloody cheek. Did you hear? What a bloody cheek.

She chucks the phone on the sofa and goes back on the internet.

JOSEPH. Put the phone back in the stand.

ALEX. I'm going to use it in a minute.

JOSEPH. Put it back.

She sighs, gets up and puts the phone back in the stand.

(*Not looking up.*) Are you aware that Suri Cruise is a fashion icon? She's the daughter of Tom Cruise and Katie Holmes.

ALEX. I know who she is.

JOSEPH. But her position of fashionista is being usurped by Gwen Stefani's eldest, Kingston Rossdale, who – (*Reading.*) 'is about to celebrate his sixth birthday wearing Moschino and Bambino Lamb, which is Gwen Stefani's new range.'

ALEX (*looking at the computer*). I could always fly to Kenya. It's much cheaper and then go overland to Kigali. I could go through Tanzania or Uganda.

JOSEPH. No.

ALEX. What's on the other side of Rwanda?

JOSEPH. Congo.

ALEX. Oh yeah. Maybe I could –

JOSEPH. No way.

ALEX. There must a cheaper way of doing this.

Pause. He looks at her. She looks up. He smiles.

I told you, I don't –

JOSEPH. We could go business class, find a great little hotel, go up north to see the gorillas, hang out for a couple of weeks, go to Lake Kivu.

ALEX (*looking back at laptop*). If I get a cheap flight then I think two grand should do it. If I stay in cheap places –

JOSEPH. It will take you about fifteen years to save that on your wages.

ALEX. If I do all the overtime I can possibly do and maybe get a bar job when all the students have gone back, then I could have enough in three months.

JOSEPH. How long are you planning on staying?

ALEX. Couple of weeks. Big fat Beverly at work says it's
    alright if I want to stay longer, she'll keep my job for me.

    Pause.

JOSEPH. You know the world-famous Central St Martins
    School of Art that we've been talking about?

ALEX. That you've been talking about.

JOSEPH. It says here that Stella McCartney studied there.

ALEX. It doesn't say that.

JOSEPH. It does. There's an article about her and her new
    designs for the Olympic team.

ALEX. No, there isn't.

JOSEPH (*reading*). 'Stella McCartney, daughter of the
    legendary Beatle Sir Paul McCartney – '

ALEX. *Grazia* would never say that.

JOSEPH. She is though.

ALEX. Everyone knows that Stella McCartney is Paul
    McCartney's daughter. And *Grazia* knows that everyone
    knows that. A schoolboy error, Joseph Potter, a schoolboy
    error. Now, give me my magazine back, I haven't finished it.

JOSEPH. You're on the internet.

ALEX. I can do both.

JOSEPH. A multi-talented girl like you really should be in
    further education. Have you thought about St Martins?

ALEX. You've got to stop going on about this.

JOSEPH. But you were so good at art. Mummy always said
    that –

ALEX. Yes, I know, but –

JOSEPH. Claire knows one of the lecturers. She said she'd be
    happy to call him and you could talk to him, ask him what
    it's like. He was a big artistic cheese in the sixties, used to
    hang out with Hockney and shit paint out of his arsehole.

    Beat.

    Just talk to him.

ALEX. Dad…

JOSEPH. And it would mean you could stay in London.

ALEX. So you keep saying.

JOSEPH. And I've heard the very famous dress designer Stella McCartney, daughter of the legendary Beatle, Sir Paul McCartney, went there.

ALEX *gets up*.

ALEX. Give it to me.

JOSEPH. Oh yeah?

ALEX. Yeah or else.

JOSEPH. Think you can take your old man, do you?

ALEX. I don't think it. I know it.

JOSEPH. That's fighting talk.

He gets up and waves the magazine at her. She moves towards him very slowly.

Ah, the slow loris technique. I hear you learnt that after many years working with Shaolin monks. Unfortunately, it is no match for the training bestowed on me by the meerkats of the Kalahari.

He gets into the position of a meerkat and then throws the magazine in the air and grabs her, pulling her to the floor and tickling her. She screams. They play-fight – laughing, screaming, squawking, running round. He holds her down and tickles her.

Repeat after me, 'I will not waste my life, I will apply for St Martins.'

ALEX (*screaming*). Never.

JOSEPH. Repeat after me. 'I will think about applying.'

ALEX. No.

JOSEPH. Repeat after me –

ALEX. Alright, alright, I will think about… ow that hurts.

He loosens his grip, she expertly takes him in a wrestling move.

Sucker. Repeat after me, 'I will do the Joseph Potter Retrospective.'

JOSEPH (*screaming*). Never.

ALEX. Repeat after me, 'I will think about doing it.'

JOSEPH. No.

ALEX. Repeat after me –

JOSEPH. Alright, alright. That's hurting. You're on my arthritic knee. Get off.

ALEX. You can't kid a kidder, kiddo. Repeat after me –

The phone rings. They freeze.

JOSEPH. It's Paul. He said –

ALEX (*letting go*). Get it then.

JOSEPH *gets up and picks the phone up.*

JOSEPH. Hello. Yes, speaking… No, I'm perfectly happy with TalkTalk, thank you. No… absolutely, yes… Bye then, bye.

ALEX. You knew it wasn't Paul, didn't you?

JOSEPH. What was it you said about kidding a kidder, kiddo?

ALEX. Dickhead.

She picks up her magazine and starts reading it while on the internet. JOSEPH *sits down and stretches out. Pause.*

JOSEPH. Seriously though –

ALEX. No.

JOSEPH. You don't know what I'm going to say yet.

ALEX. I do.

JOSEPH. I don't want you to waste what –

ALEX. And I want you to leave me alone to make my own decisions.

JOSEPH. Even if I think they're the wrong decisions, like doing some shitty job even though you don't have to and running away from King's after all that work you put in to get there. Then pissing off to Kigali on some vague notion about the motherland when you don't know the first thing about it and you're as green as a bloody gooseberry.

ALEX. It says in here – (*Picking up Rwanda guidebook.*) 'I have travelled as a lone woman…'

JOSEPH. You need to think about it. You need to –

ALEX. I'm going to go to the Kigali Genocide Memorial and if I'm there for a Thursday I can go to this event called 'One in a Million' where a survivor speaks and they show the film *Straw Dogs*.

JOSEPH. *Straw Dogs* is a thriller set in Cornwall.

ALEX. *Shooting Dogs,* I mean *Shooting Dogs*.

JOSEPH. Sounds lovely.

ALEX. Then I'm going south to Butare to the National Museum. It's supposed to be amazing and then back to Kigali and then north to my village to –

JOSEPH. I don't know why we're even talking about this. You're not going.

ALEX. What?

JOSEPH. I forbid you to go.

She snorts.

You're going to be disappointed. Whatever you've pictured in your head is wrong. You're going to see things that are going to hurt you. You're going to get hurt and you'll be thousands of miles away and I won't be able to help you.

ALEX. I don't need your help.

JOSEPH. You have no idea what you're getting in to.

ALEX. I do. I know all about it.

She goes out. Pause. JOSEPH sits on the sofa, listening to her banging about upstairs. She comes down the stairs and kicks open the door with an armful of books.

(Reading and throwing them onto the floor.) The Rwanda Crisis: History of Genocide, Left to Tell: One Woman's Story of Surviving the Rwandan Holocaust, Miracle in Kigali, Season of Blood, We Wish to Inform You That Tomorrow We Will Be Killed With Our Families, A Thousand Hills: Rwanda's Rebirth and the Man Who Dreamed It.

JOSEPH. Where did you –

ALEX. Amazon.

She puts on a CD of Rwandan music.

JOSEPH. When did –

ALEX. When I was in my shitty bedsit wondering who the fuck I was.

The music plays. He looks at her. A long time. He turns the music off.

JOSEPH. If you go, you'll have to find somewhere else to live.

ALEX. What?

JOSEPH. I can't collude with something I think will damage you.

ALEX. You can't –

JOSEPH. I'm sorry, but –

ALEX. I don't believe this.

JOSEPH. It's for your own good.

ALEX. Is it?

JOSEPH. You're too young. You're just too –

ALEX. You were nineteen when you first went away.

JOSEPH. We're not talking about me.

ALEX. To Vietnam.

Beat.

JOSEPH. And I'm not exactly an advert for global travel, am I?

ALEX. It's a holiday. That's all. Just a holiday.

JOSEPH. It's not a fucking holiday, Alex, it's a massive fucking life-changing fucking decision.

Pause.

ALEX. I want to know who I am.

JOSEPH. You're Alex. You're Alex from Hampstead who won at place at King's. You're my daughter. You're mine and Meg's lovely clever beautiful daughter and I –

ALEX. Sometimes when I think of going back, I feel like I could run there. Like I'm being called back or something. I know it sounds ridiculous, I know, but I –

JOSEPH. I understand, but –

ALEX. And sometimes I don't give a shit about any of it and I just want to stack shelves for the rest of my life.

Scene Five

ALEX *has the lighting box on and a set of negatives on it. It is on the floor with the light on. A bag of Scrabble letters are spread over the floor. She is sitting motionless on the sofa. JOSEPH returns home.*

JOSEPH. Why aren't you at work? (*Opens curtains.*) And why are you sitting in the dark? Are you going Goth again? Because if you are, can I remind you of the incident in 2006 with the crimpers and an unnecessary call-out of the fire brigade?

He sees the light box on the floor and the negatives.

Put these away.

Pause. She doesn't move.

Did you hear me?

Pause.

Alex.

Beat.

Get up.

*She doesn't move. He puts his bags down and starts
gathering everything up.*

ALEX. I didn't know whether to sort through them
chronologically or by continent. I thought about going through
them alphabetically, country by country. In the end, I settled
on a random approach. I thought that would work just as well
as alphabetically, which is kind of random anyway and doing
it randomly was kind of elegant, you know, like the work, a
nice echo of your work, so I used the Scrabble letters.

JOSEPH. What are you –

ALEX. Last week I pulled out U, C, E and I. I did Uganda,
Cambodia, Ethiopia and Israel. I checked them for damage
and I put the ones I thought were the best at the front for
when you show Paul.

JOSEPH. I told you I'm not –

ALEX. And yesterday I did Vietnam and today was Zimbabwe.
Every day I've been preparing myself to pull out an R. I kept
thinking it's bound to be today, that R, it's only worth one
point. I was sure this morning it had to be an R, but I got a Z.
All that stuff they taught us at school about probability is
obviously total shit, because a Z is ten points and there's
only one. I couldn't find Zimbabwe for ages. It wasn't where
it should have been. I was getting pissed off, a bit creeped
out down in the cellar and then right at the back, under
everything else, I found it. I brought it up here super-quick,
because I had to get back to work and my supervisor Darren
is an uptight prick and I'd wasted twenty minutes looking for
it and when I opened it, I saw that you'd put the Rwanda
shots in the Zimbabwe box.

JOSEPH *opens the door to go out with everything in his
hands.*

Why did you do that?

JOSEPH. Alex, I –

ALEX. Why are the Rwanda negatives in the Zimbabwe box?

JOSEPH. I have no idea.

ALEX. Don't you?

JOSEPH. Maybe your mother put them there. You should get back to work.

ALEX. I feel sick. I feel sick to my stomach.

JOSEPH. You shouldn't have gone down there.

She shows him a Sunday Times *with the year's best photos of 1994.*

ALEX. I found this as well.

Beat.

All the other entries are quite disgusting, aren't they? And here I am sandwiched between – (*Looking*.) a Palestinian with her leg blown off and a man with his face melting in the – (*Reading*.) New South Wales bushfires. Lovely.

JOSEPH. I've told you I don't want to do that bloody exhibition. I've been very clear how I feel and –

ALEX. Why was my photo cropped?

Beat.

Why did you crop my photo?

JOSEPH. What are you –

ALEX. My photo. It's been cropped.

Beat.

Well?

JOSEPH. I didn't crop anything. I –

ALEX. That's funny, because the original isn't the same as this groundbreaking, world-celebrated, award-winning one here – (*Indicates magazine*.)

Pause.

JOSEPH. The photo-editor did it.

ALEX. Why?

JOSEPH. Because it was stronger. Now, give me that – (*Indicates magazine*.)

Pause.

ALEX. Who's the boy?

Beat.

The boy in the church with me and the bodies.

She gets up and takes the light box out of his arms, finds the Rwandan shot, plugs the light box in and shows him. He walks away. She pulls him back.

(*Shows him on light box.*) The boy in the corner looking straight at you.

Beat.

Look.

Pause.

Who is he?

Beat.

You said there was no one else left.

JOSEPH. There wasn't.

ALEX. You said the whole village was slaughtered.

JOSEPH. They were.

ALEX. You said my family was killed. That I was the only one that survived.

JOSEPH. Yes.

Beat.

ALEX. So?

JOSEPH. Alex, listen, it's not –

ALEX. Who is he?

JOSEPH. I went in the church, I saw the bodies, I saw you and I took the shot. I heard the Interahamwe coming. I picked you up and ran.

ALEX. And you didn't notice him when you walked in?

JOSEPH. It was a bloodbath, there were hundreds of corpses just lying –

ALEX. He's looking right at you.

JOSEPH. I couldn't –

ALEX. How could you not have seen him?

JOSEPH. I –

ALEX. You must have.

Beat.

You must have.

JOSEPH. Okay, Alex, okay.

He nods.

ALEX. Shit.

JOSEPH. Yeah.

Pause.

I saw him. As I was leaving with you, I saw him standing in the corner.

ALEX. Why didn't you – ?

JOSEPH. I couldn't carry you both.

ALEX. But if you'd –

JOSEPH. There was no time. The Interahamwe were coming back.

Beat.

I had to make a decision.

ALEX. Right.

JOSEPH. I had to choose. Do you understand?

ALEX. Yeah.

Beat.

How did you choose?

JOSEPH. You were smaller.

Pause.

If I could have taken you both, I would have. If I could have –

ALEX. Why didn't you tell me?

JOSEPH. There was no point.

ALEX. Why?

> JOSEPH *looks at her. She knows. Pause.*

> Are you sure?

> *He nods.*

> But he might have escaped, he might have –

JOSEPH. The Interahamwe came back.

ALEX. But you didn't see what happened to him? He might have –

JOSEPH. He's dead.

ALEX. But –

JOSEPH. They killed him.

ALEX. But he might have –

JOSEPH. I heard them.

Scene Six

ALEX *is lying on the sofa in her pyjamas watching television. Her phone rings. She ignores it.* JOSEPH *comes in with shopping and his portfolio under his arm.*

ALEX. Did you tell her to call me?

JOSEPH. Who?

> *Beat.* ALEX *looks at him.*

> I bumped into Trish in Waitrose and she was talking about Lily and I said maybe, if she wanted to, if she felt like it, she could give you a call.

ALEX. She's fucking stalking me now.

JOSEPH. I thought you could do with some support.

Beat.

I really think you should think about –

ALEX. No.

Pause.

JOSEPH. Why don't you go back to work?

ALEX. I don't want to.

JOSEPH. It'll be good for you.

ALEX. You've changed your tune.

JOSEPH. It'll keep you busy. I think it's –

ALEX. I haven't been in for three weeks and I've ignored all Darren the prick's messages and big fat Beverly's emails so I think it's safe to assume that ship has sailed.

JOSEPH. Right. Okay.

Pause.

(*Gets out an almond croissant.*) I got you this.

ALEX. Eaten already.

JOSEPH. It's from that stall, the one with the French boy you used to like.

Beat.

Alex…

ALEX (*turns the television up*). I'm busy.

Pause.

JOSEPH. Alex, turn it off.

ALEX. I'm not going back to King's and I'm not going to St Martins. And I'm not running off to the motherland either, so I don't think there's much to talk about, do you?

Pause.

JOSEPH. What are you doing for the rest of the day?

ALEX (*lies back on the sofa*). This.

JOSEPH. You can help me then.

JOSEPH *opens the portfolio with prints in it*. ALEX *flicks through the channels.*

(*Sits down next to her.*) The first room's going to be divided into three categories; terror, famine and genocide –

ALEX. Oh, stop it, you're making me all sentimental.

JOSEPH. It's a gimmick.

ALEX. You don't say.

JOSEPH. Makes it easier for people to navigate round.

Beat.

I wanted to do it chronologically, but when Paul and I met the curator, Greta, who's German, she said something about 'thematic butter'. I don't know, maybe something got lost in translation –

ALEX. Whatever.

JOSEPH. I'm doing what you wanted, Alex.

ALEX. Wanted. Past tense.

JOSEPH. Listen, I would have been quite happy sitting around in my pants all day and shooting the odd wedding.

ALEX. I don't give a shit.

JOSEPH. Give me a break, will you, I'm trying –

She turns up the television. They sit in silence.

Turn it down.

She turns it up.

I said turn it down.

She turns the volume up. He takes it from her and turns it off. She grabs it off him and turns it back on. He waits a few seconds, grabs it, turns it off, goes to the door and throws the remote outside into the hall.

ALEX. You see these – (*Pointing to legs.*) They're called legs.
They move when my brain tells them to. They can walk out
there and get that remote control that you have petulantly
thrown out of the door possibly broken rendering the TV
obsolete.

She gets up and gets the remote.

They make TVs without buttons so you can't change
channels without it and when the remote is lost or broken or
thrown out into the hall by a deranged father, they're pleased
because they know you'll buy a new telly. That's how they
get you. One minute you're in Currys asking for a new
remote control and the next you're at home on the sofa in
front of a wall-sized Bang & Olufsen, with a bag of Percy
Pigs and the director's cut of *Blade Runner*. Bastards.

Pause.

JOSEPH. I love Percy Pigs.

ALEX *tuts*.

Your mother used to –

ALEX. Which mother? The first dead one or the second dead
one?

JOSEPH. Alex…

ALEX. Two dead mothers before I'm twenty. I really must have
been a shit in my past life.

JOSEPH. Come on…

ALEX. Maybe I was a serial rapist.

JOSEPH. Don't be silly.

ALEX. Is this conversation finished?

JOSEPH. I don't know why you're being like this.

ALEX. Don't you?

JOSEPH. No.

ALEX. You must be thicker than I thought.

Beat.

JOSEPH. Would you rather I'd left you behind?

Beat.

ALEX. I think I would, yeah.

JOSEPH. Then you really are an idiot.

ALEX. Whatever.

JOSEPH. Did you read those books about the genocide?

ALEX. Yeah.

JOSEPH. Doesn't sound like it.

ALEX. I did.

JOSEPH. Well, show some respect for the people who were left behind.

ALEX. I do have resp–

JOSEPH. All those poor bastards who would have done anything to have your life.

ALEX. I think I must have survivor's guilt.

JOSEPH. And I think you're an ungrateful little cunt.

Scene Seven

JOSEPH *is sitting in the dark. Laptop surrounded by prints. He shuts the laptop down, closes his eyes.* ALEX *comes down in her pyjamas. She watches him.*

ALEX. I can't sleep.

JOSEPH. There's some lavender oil by my bed.

ALEX. Had some.

JOSEPH. Try the Kalms in the bathroom cabinet.

ALEX. I've taken two already.

JOSEPH. There's valium in my sock drawer if you want it.

ALEX. Maybe I'll just have a drink of water.

Pause. She stands in the doorway.

When are you going to bed?

JOSEPH. Soon.

Beat.

ALEX. Can I sleep in with you?

Beat.

JOSEPH. Sure.

Beat.

ALEX. I'll see you up there.

JOSEPH. Okay.

She stands in the doorway and looks at him. She walks in and sits on the sofa. Pause.

ALEX. About earlier…

JOSEPH. It doesn't matter.

ALEX. It does.

JOSEPH. It's fine.

ALEX. I'm sorry.

JOSEPH. You don't have to –

ALEX. I don't know what's going on with me at the moment. I don't know –

JOSEPH. Forget it. We both said things –

ALEX. It was my fault, it –

JOSEPH. No father should ever call his daughter a –

ALEX. Well, if she's being one –

JOSEPH. You weren't.

Pause. She gets up.

ALEX. Do you want anything from the kitchen?

He shakes his head. She goes to the kitchen. He sits and stares into space. She comes back with a drink of water and a glass of whisky. He stares into space.

Dad?

She hands it to him. Beat.

Are we okay?

Beat.

JOSEPH. Yeah.

ALEX. Are you sure?

JOSEPH. Yeah.

ALEX. Are you sure?

JOSEPH. Yes, I'm sure.

ALEX. But are you sure you're sure?

JOSEPH. Yes, I'm sure I'm sure.

ALEX. But are you sure you're sure you're sure?

JOSEPH. I'll see you upstairs in a minute.

She hugs him and kisses him on the cheek. Beat. He pulls her to sit down on the chair with him. She squeezes in next to him in the armchair he is sitting in.

ALEX. Christ, you are such a fatso.

He puts his arms round her.

JOSEPH. You know that I love you very much, don't –

ALEX. Shit, you're not ill are you –

JOSEPH. No, why would I –

ALEX. That's the classic terminal-illness opener, you should know that. You should –

JOSEPH. There's nothing wrong with me.

ALEX. Bloody hell. Good. God. I don't think I could take losing another one.

Beat.

This is not very comfortable. I think my arse has grown.

She gets up.

JOSEPH. Alex, I've had an email.

ALEX. Yeah?

JOSEPH. Earlier, this evening, I got this email –

ALEX. Okay.

JOSEPH. I was going to wait till morning.

ALEX. What is it?

JOSEPH. It's from someone in Rwanda.

ALEX. Who?

Beat.

Who is it?

JOSEPH. I don't want to get your hopes up, but –

ALEX. Who?

JOSEPH. I don't want you to –

ALEX. Bloody hell, just –

JOSEPH. It's from a man called Simon.

ALEX. Who's Simon?

JOSEPH. He says he's your brother.

Beat.

I was going to tell you in the morning. I thought you were asleep. I didn't want to –

ALEX. What does it say?

JOSEPH. Not much, just that he's been trying to find you and –

She gets his laptop and turns it on.

ALEX. What's your password? (*Tapping the keys.*) Why's this so fucking slow –

JOSEPH. Just listen.

ALEX (*hitting it*). Fuck it.

JOSEPH. Stop. (*Takes it from her.*) Listen to me. It's really important, that you –

ALEX. How did he find you?

Beat.

JOSEPH. He saw the photograph.

ALEX. What's that got –

JOSEPH. It's him.

Beat.

The boy.

Beat.

ALEX. But you said he was –

JOSEPH. I know. I thought… But he says he remembers the day. He says he remembers you and remembers seeing me with my camera.

ALEX. Fucking hell.

JOSEPH. I know.

ALEX. Fucking hell.

Beat.

Does he want to see me?

JOSEPH. Yes.

ALEX. Good. God, that would've been an anticlimax, wouldn't it?

Beat.

JOSEPH. You know, he only says that he's your brother.

ALEX. Yeah.

JOSEPH. He says it.

Beat.

We need to be a little cautious, that's all. Just because he says it, that doesn't mean –

ALEX. Why would he –

JOSEPH. Millions of people have seen that shot. You know, it's very –

ALEX. And how many of them know there's a little boy that's been edited out of it?

JOSEPH. I think we need to be careful, that's all. Let's not rush into anything. We're both a bit fraught, you know, it would be easy to get caught up in this.

ALEX. I'm going to email him now.

JOSEPH. We need to take care, you know, tread carefully, we don't know anything about this man, he could be –

ALEX. We do. We know that he's the boy that you left behind.

ACT TWO

Scene Eight

ALEX *and* SIMON *stand opposite looking at each other. His bags on the floor.*

ALEX. Do you like music?

SIMON. Of course.

ALEX. What kind of music do you like?

SIMON. Hip hop.

ALEX. Do you?

SIMON. Do you?

ALEX. Not really. I like alternative stuff, indie stuff, you know, stuff outside the mainstream, unusual stuff like… I don't know, just… it doesn't really matter. Yeah, I like some hip hop, I suppose.

SIMON. 50 Cent?

ALEX. No, not 50 Cent.

SIMON. Lil Wayne?

ALEX. No, not really, no. I mean, I don't really like that kind of hip hop, not really. I don't –

SIMON. Celine Dion?

ALEX *laughs.* SIMON *looks at her.*

ALEX. Did you eat on the plane?

SIMON. Yes.

Beat.

ALEX. What did you have?

SIMON. Beef in the juice of tomatoes.

ALEX. Was it nice?

SIMON. Yes.

ALEX. What else did you have?

SIMON. Rice.

ALEX. And for pudding?

SIMON. Pudding?

ALEX. Dessert.

SIMON. A pastry.

ALEX. Did you like it?

SIMON. Yes.

Beat.

ALEX. Did you sleep at all?

SIMON. Yes.

ALEX. Good.

Beat.

I never sleep on planes. It's so uncomfortable. It always smells funny. I think it's all the farting. You know, because of the high altitude, everyone… you know…

Pause.

Do you want something else? To eat?

SIMON. Thank you, no.

Pause.

ALEX. When I went to Russia, we were given peas and mashed potato for our meal. That was it.

SIMON. It sounds very delicious.

ALEX. No, it wasn't… I mean…

Beat.

Shall I show you to your room?

SIMON. No, thank you.

Pause. He looks at her. The door slams.

JOSEPH (*shouting from outside*). Oi-oi! Got some supplies for our guest from Africa! Africa! (*Kicks open the door.*) Give us a hand, you lazy... (*Sees* SIMON.) Oh God, sorry, I didn't realise... I thought you were going to call from the airport... I thought...

SIMON (*offers his hand*). It is a pleasure to meet you.

JOSEPH. Right, yes, and you – (*Tries to hold his hand out, but can't.*) Hold on, let me get rid of this lot.

He struggles to puts the bags down. SIMON *and* ALEX *stand awkwardly in silence.*

(*Offers his hand.*) Hi, Simon, I'm Joseph, Alex's dad.

SIMON. Yes, it is wonderful to meet you and thank you for inviting me.

JOSEPH. No, no, the pleasure is all ours.

SIMON. It is a great honour to be welcomed into your home.

JOSEPH. Yes, well, okay, thank you for coming.

SIMON. Thank you for the invitation.

JOSEPH. Right, okay, so...

Beat.

Have you had a drink? Has my daughter offered you a drink?

SIMON (*indicating water*). Yes, thank you.

JOSEPH. And how was the flight?

SIMON. Very comfortable, thank you.

Pause.

JOSEPH. And you've met Alex.

SIMON. Yes.

Pause.

JOSEPH. What did you eat on the plane?

Beat.

SIMON. Beef in juice of a tomato and rice. And a pastry. It was very enjoyable.

Beat.

JOSEPH (*to* ALEX). Remember when we went to Moscow? We had –

ALEX. I told him.

SIMON. Delicious.

Pause.

JOSEPH. How did you get from the airport?

SIMON. The train and two buses.

JOSEPH. I would've picked you up. I said in the email that I'd pick you up.

SIMON. It was no trouble.

JOSEPH. You should have called.

SIMON. It was no trouble.

JOSEPH. But still, if you'd –

ALEX. Dad.

Pause.

JOSEPH. How did you know which buses to get?

SIMON. I asked the people at the bus stop and the bus officer.

JOSEPH. The bus officer?

SIMON. Yes.

Pause. SIMON *stares at* ALEX.

JOSEPH. Right, well, shall we show to your room?

SIMON. No, thank you.

JOSEPH. What about some food?

SIMON. No, thank you.

JOSEPH. We could go out. Let's do that.

SIMON. No, thank you.

JOSEPH. God, no, sorry, of course, you probably want to rest or shower or something. How long was the flight?

Beat. SIMON *stares at* ALEX. ALEX *looks at* JOSEPH.

SIMON (*staring at* ALEX). It was seven hours.

JOSEPH. Right and did you have to change?

Beat. SIMON *stares at* ALEX. ALEX *looks at* JOSEPH.

SIMON (*staring at* ALEX). At Brussels.

JOSEPH. Yeah, of course. Bloody Belgians. It was all their fault in the first place, wasn't it? The… you know, colonising Rwanda and all that, bloody bastards. Good chocolate though, Belgium chocolate, bloody good chocolate. Fucking good chocolate actually. And the waffles. The waffles are really terrific too.

Pause. SIMON *looks at* ALEX. *A long time.*

ALEX *starts giggling.*

ALEX (*giggling*). I'm sorry. This is so weird. This is so –

JOSEPH. Alex…

ALEX. Sorry.

She stops. She looks at SIMON.

(*To* JOSEPH.) Do you think we look like each other? (*To* SIMON.) Do you?

SIMON (*singing*).
    We are family,
    I got my sister here with me.

ALEX *and* JOSEPH *look at each other.*

    Get up everybody and sing.
    We are family.
    I got my sister here with me.
    Get up everybody and sing.

Pause. They all look at each other.

I changed the words a little.

Beat. ALEX *starts laughing.*

You look like our mother.

Scene Nine

ALEX *and* SIMON *arrive home. The living room is empty.*

ALEX (*calling*). Dad? Dad?

> *She opens the door and jumps over the sofa.* SIMON *follows her in.*

Dad! We're home.

SIMON (*reading from a guide to London*). 'During the Great Frost of 1683 to 1684, the worst frost recorded in England, the Thames was completely frozen for two months, with the ice reaching a thickness of eleven inches, twenty-eight centimetres, in London.' Alex, did you know this?

ALEX. Yeah, they used to have frost fairs on the river. (*Shouting.*) Dad!

> *She gets out her phone and dials.* SIMON *looks at the index and finds the right page.*

Where are you?... Can't you hear me calling you?... God, alright, keep your hair on. Just wanted to tell you we're back. Are you coming down?

SIMON (*reading*). The frost fair of 1814 began on 1st February and lasted four days. An elephant was led across the river below Blackfriars Bridge.

ALEX. Have you ever seen an elephant?

SIMON. Of course.

ALEX. I didn't know there are elephants in Rwanda.

SIMON. No, but there are televisions.

ALEX. Oh yeah, sorry, what a bell-end.

SIMON. What is a –

JOSEPH *comes down the stairs.*

ALEX. Look out, here comes the grumpy old git.

JOSEPH *comes in the room wearing his dressing gown and smoking a joint.* SIMON *stands up.*

SIMON. Good afternoon, Joseph.

JOSEPH (*waves at him to sit down*). You make me feel like Princess Margaret when you do that.

SIMON *looks at* ALEX. *He sits down.*

ALEX. We've been to the London Eye.

JOSEPH. Oh yeah?

SIMON. It was fantastic.

ALEX. Have you been asleep?

JOSEPH. No.

SIMON. You are still in your sleeping clothing.

JOSEPH (*looks down*). Oh my God, you're right.

ALEX (*embarrassed*). Alright, Dad.

Pause.

JOSEPH. I've been trying to sort out the study.

ALEX. Have you?

JOSEPH. It's a bloody disgrace.

ALEX. It's a long time since you went in there.

JOSEPH. I thought I might as well start using it again. You know, keep everything contained rather than spreading it all over the place, try and keep it under control. You know what I'm like once I get started, everything turns into a bloody tsunami, you know what Meg always used to say about –

ALEX. How's it all going?

JOSEPH. Fine.

ALEX. What are you up to?

JOSEPH. Apartheid, '84 to '87.

ALEX. Are you enjoying it?

JOSEPH. Oh yes, shits and giggles all the way.

Pause.

SIMON. It must make you very proud.

Beat.

To have this exhibition. For everyone to see.

Pause.

ALEX. Simon told me that I used to be called Frances.

Beat.

JOSEPH. That's nice.

SIMON. Yes, but Alex is also very nice too.

JOSEPH. After the explorer Alexandra David-Neel. She went to Tibet about a hundred years before Richard Gere and his hamster.

Pause.

My head is killing me. And my neck. I think I've strained it or something. I feel like I've been run over. These glasses are shit as well. I feel like a myopic piece of bloody roadkill.

Beat.

SIMON. I think perhaps I might go upstairs to read this book.

JOSEPH. Stay. I'm being a twat.

Beat. SIMON *looks at* ALEX.

(*Getting up.*) I've got to get on. Paul's on my back like a premature baby marmoset and I can't take a piss without sauerkraut Greta sending me an email about Die Unmenschlichkeit von Mann.

ALEX. Stay a bit, Dad. Take a break.

Beat.

Please.

He sits down. Pause.

SIMON. We went to the Globe.

JOSEPH. Right. How was it?

SIMON. We took part in a tour.

ALEX (*laughing*). Simon asked the tour leader if she was
related to Shakespeare. Simon knows loads of Shakespeare.
He even knows *Timon of Athens*. Who the hell knows that?

SIMON. I was in *Othello* when I was at university. I started a
group.

JOSEPH. It's an amazing part, Othello, it's –

SIMON. I was Iago.

Beat.

JOSEPH. Right.

ALEX. I was Titania at school. Wasn't I, Dad?

JOSEPH. Yep, it was abridged though.

ALEX. Still Shakespeare.

JOSEPH. And it was a musical.

ALEX. Yeah, but it's still Shakespeare.

JOSEPH. Oberon came on to 'Purple Haze' and looked like a
lesbian Gordon Brown. Me and Meg couldn't stop laughing.

Pause.

What did you study?

SIMON. Tourism.

JOSEPH. I suppose that helps with your job.

SIMON. Yes and my languages as well.

ALEX. Tell him all the languages you speak.

SIMON. French, English, Swahili, Kinyawanda and a little Norwegian.

JOSEPH. Norwegian?

SIMON. My sponsor is Norwegian.

ALEX. He had a sponsor who paid for him to go to school and university.

SIMON. Angelique.

ALEX. He met her in the street. Just started talking to her when he was...

SIMON. Eight. She was working for an NGO.

ALEX. And she financially supported him.

JOSEPH. Like we did with... (*Looks at* ALEX.)

ALEX. Lakshmi.

JOSEPH. Lakshmi, of course. We used to sponsor an Indian girl.

SIMON. And how old is she now?

JOSEPH *looks at* ALEX. ALEX *shrugs*.

JOSEPH. Meg did it. Meg started it all. It was... I mean, she was... Meg's project. Not project, you know, Meg thought it would be a nice thing to do.

Pause.

So, what exactly do you do, you know, day in day out?

SIMON. I give tours of the church, explaining what happened. I tell them my story, I answer the questions, and I stop people having their photos taken in front of the skulls.

JOSEPH *laughs*.

ALEX. Who goes to the church?

SIMON. Survivors, relatives, some tourists before they go to see the gorillas.

JOSEPH. Gorillas and genocide. Beats Alton Towers, I suppose.

ALEX. We're going to go to Westminster Cathedral tomorrow. You can come if you like.

JOSEPH. I've got a meeting.

SIMON. We are going to Madame Tussauds as well.

ALEX. I keep telling him it's shit, but he won't listen.

SIMON. I want to stand with David Beckham.

JOSEPH. You used to love Madame Tussauds.

ALEX. Did I?

JOSEPH. You used to kiss Ronan Keating.

ALEX. God, did I?

JOSEPH. Yep. I used to lift you up and Meg used to say – (*Irish accent*.) 'I love you, Alex.' (*To* SIMON.) Alex's mum was brilliant at accents, wasn't she? She was a fantastic mimic as well, really funny. She used to do your headteacher perfectly, didn't she?

ALEX. Yeah.

Beat.

Do you want me to get you a coffee? You look tired.

JOSEPH. There's a bottle of Glenfiddich on top of the fridge.

ALEX. I'll make a proper one with the machine or I could make you a smoothie.

JOSEPH. The whisky'll do.

ALEX. Dad…

JOSEPH (*getting up*). Forget it, I'll get it myself.

ALEX. No, it's alright, I'll go.

JOSEPH. Bring the bottle through.

She gets up.

ALEX (*to* SIMON). Do you want anything?

SIMON *shakes his head.*

Why don't you come and see? (*To* JOSEPH.) He hardly eats anything.

SIMON. No thanks.

ALEX. Come and look in the fridge.

JOSEPH. Why don't you leave the poor bastard alone?

ALEX. I just want to make sure –

JOSEPH. He's a grown man.

ALEX. Okay, okay. Glenfiddich it is then.

She stands in the doorway. She turns and goes. Pause.

JOSEPH. Why are you here?

SIMON. You invited me.

Pause.

I have been waiting a long time.

JOSEPH. I know.

SIMON. I have been patient.

JOSEPH. I know.

SIMON. Yes.

JOSEPH. It wasn't the right time.

Beat.

Meg was ill… and…

Beat.

Then when she died, it was –

SIMON. I understand.

JOSEPH. Alex had her GCSEs.

SIMON. Yes.

JOSEPH. And then her A-levels and then she was applying for university… well, there was never a right time.

Pause.

SIMON. Joseph?

Beat.

I forgive you.

Scene Ten

ALEX *and* SIMON *on the sofa. The television is on. A heap of old family photo albums lie on the floor.* SIMON *is looking through one of the albums.* ALEX *points.*

ALEX. That's Granny Harris. Mum's mum. She's dead now. What do you want to watch?

He flicks through the album and shrugs.

What about *Grand Designs*?

She looks over and points.

My Marilyn Manson phase. (*Flicks channels.*) *Rasta Mouse*?

The front door bangs shut.

(*Getting up and looking out window.*) He didn't say he was going out. How rude.

ALEX *sits back down and points at a picture.*

That was at Whitstable. Mum made Dad come out with us for the day. I remember he was really pissed off, being an angry old bastard, as usual.

She looks at another.

This was when he got a lifetime-achievement thing at the World Press Awards. Mum wanted a party to celebrate, but he didn't want any fuss. The next day, she found him hiding in the cupboard. He was in bed for a year. They said he had post-traumatic stress disorder.

Beat.

Mum wanted him to keep seeing the psychiatrist, but he wouldn't. And as soon as he felt better he went to Afghanistan, which was really –

SIMON. I went to a psychiatrist.

ALEX. Did you?

SIMON. When I tried to kill myself.

ALEX. Shit, Simon, I'm –

SIMON. Sister Innocence found me. They told me to leave the school.

ALEX. Bloody hell.

SIMON. Angelique found him and paid for me to see him.

ALEX. And what did he say?

SIMON. He said he watched the Interahamwe disembowel his children and that he wanted to kill himself also.

Beat. He looks down at the photos.

ALEX. How long did you see him for?

SIMON. It does not matter.

ALEX. It must have been –

SIMON. It does not matter.

ALEX. But –

SIMON. It does not matter.

Pause. She reaches over and takes the book and starts looking through it. Silence. She stops and looks at a photograph. SIMON *looks too.*

And what is this?

ALEX. My first day at primary school. That's my uncle Sylvester standing next to me. Dad was away, so Mum asked her brother to come over to take the photo.

He looks for a long time.

And this was when Mum taught me to swim. See that swimsuit, it had the Teletubbies on it, which were like, massive here when I was little. That purple one was supposed to be gay because he had a handbag. I loved that swimsuit so much and I used to wear it to bed. I remember I even tried to wear it to school. In the end, Mum had to hide it.

She turns the page.

And this one, was Mum's fiftieth, we had a surprise party. It was brilliant. I remember her face when she walked in, it was –

He closes the album and puts it down. Pause. She looks at him. He picks up the album, looks at it, pulls back the cellophane, takes the photo out and rips it in half and drops it on the floor.

What the –

He takes another out and does the same.

What are you doing –

She reaches over to take the album from him. He jumps off the sofa and takes the album with him. He tears out a page.

Don't.

He rips it to pieces.

Stop it. Fucking stop it.

She tries to pull the album away from him. He tears another page out and throws the album across the room. She gets down on the floor and frantically starts picking up the photos. He goes out. He goes upstairs. We hear him move, banging open the door to JOSEPH's *study.* ALEX *goes to the door. Sounds of drawers being pulled open and emptied. She runs up the stairs.*

(*Off.*) Stop it. What are you doing? Don't.

Get out of here. He'll go mad if he –

Don't. Put that back.

Sounds of a scuffle. ALEX *cries out. Sounds of footsteps on the steps. Still sounds of ransacking upstairs.* ALEX *enters. She goes to the phone. It's not on the stand. She frantically looks everywhere for it.*

Fuck. Fuck.

She picks up the cushions trying to find it. She goes to her bag and looks for her mobile. She can't find it. She empties her bag on the floor, finds her phone, dials JOSEPH. *His answerphone.*

(*Chucking the phone down.*) Fuck it.

SIMON *stands in the doorway. The* Sunday Times *magazine in his hands. He goes to her.*

SIMON (*pointing at the photograph*). This is Odette. She
delivered all of us into the world. She was our mother's
childhood friend. She married a Hutu called Anton. They
lived next door to our house. Anton killed her first. When he
found us in the church, he ripped off our mother's dress and
gave it to his sister who was standing next to him who tried
it on. Then he pulled our mother onto the floor and raped her
in front of everyone she had known for her whole life. They
chopped our father's ankles so he could not move and held
his eyes open so he must watch.

Beat.

Do you remember that?

Beat.

I remember our father begging for mercy and they ripped out
his tongue. I remember our brother Gerard running away and
his teacher arriving back in the church wearing his shoes,
which were covered in blood. I remember hiding under dead
bodies, covering your mouth so you would not scream, blood
running down my face and how warm it felt and wondering
whose it was, because I knew it was not mine. I remember
them laughing and the smell of the alcohol when they had
gone. I remember pushing my way out and letting you go
and watching you crawl over the bodies of our family and
our friends. I remember you reaching our mother and pulling
at her breast to feed you, because she still had the milk. I
remember knowing that nothing would ever be the same. I
remember waiting for them to come back and to kill us. I
remember seeing a white man in the church and thinking it
was God.

Pause.

I thought your father was God.

Beat.

And he had come to save us both.

Scene Eleven

JOSEPH *is drinking coffee and trying to text on his phone. He tuts.* ALEX *walks in wearing her pants and T-shirt, eating a bowl of Corn Flakes.*

JOSEPH. Put some fucking clothes on, will you?

ALEX. Good morning, Alex, and how are you today? Very well thanks, Dad. How did you sleep? Like a baby, thanks for asking. And how are you, Dad? I'm in a terrible mood as per usual.

JOSEPH. And how did you sleep, Dad? Like I was trapped in some William Blake pit of despair and Throbbing Gristle were playing in my skull, thanks for asking.

She sits down. JOSEPH *still texting.*

I've got to see someone about taking the show to New York and I'm expecting some prints to be couriered over, you need to be in at two to sign for them.

ALEX. We're going to the Royal Observatory this afternoon.

JOSEPH. Go tomorrow.

ALEX. I wanted to take Simon to Brighton tomorrow. I was going to ask if I could borrow the car.

Beat.

So, can I?

JOSEPH. What?

ALEX. Borrow the car?

Beat.

JOSEPH. How long is he going to be with us?

ALEX. I don't know.

JOSEPH. How long's his visa?

ALEX. Three months.

Beat.

Is there a problem?

JOSEPH. I'd like to get a bit of normality back.

Beat.

I'd like you to start thinking about what you're going to do.

ALEX. God, not this again.

JOSEPH. Your life can't just be endless trips to Thorpe Park and *The Lion King*, Alex.

ALEX. Tate Britain and the John Soane's Museum. So fuck off.

JOSEPH. You know what I mean.

ALEX. He's only been here a month.

JOSEPH. Yes and you've got some important decisions to make regarding your future and you're acting like some lovesick adolescent.

ALEX. I'm going back to work next week actually.

JOSEPH. Not at Sainsbury's –

ALEX. Yeah, I spoke to Beverly and she –

SIMON *enters.*

SIMON. Good morning, Joseph, and how are you?

JOSEPH. Brilliant.

SIMON. And how are you on this marvellous beautiful morning, Alex?

ALEX *laughs.* JOSEPH*'s phone beeps. He reads a text.*

JOSEPH. Make sure you're in for two when the courier arrives.

ALEX. But –

He slams the living-room door.

SIMON. What is wrong with Joseph?

ALEX. Fuck knows.

SIMON. Alex, you know I do not like the swearing.

ALEX *tuts.*

It is not polite.

ALEX *rolls her eyes*.

And you must put some clothes on.

ALEX. Alright, Dad.

SIMON. This is not respectable.

ALEX. God, half of Africa walks round with their boobs hanging out.

SIMON. It is not right to walk around like –

ALEX. Bloody hell, patriarchy is alive and well in NW3. I never thought I'd have two men telling me what to do in this house.

SIMON (*getting his book out and pen*). Spell it, please.

ALEX. P–A–T–R–I–A–R–C–H–Y.

SIMON (*writing it down in his book*). Slow. Slow.

ALEX (*slowly*). P–A–T–R–I–A–R–C–H–Y.

SIMON (*reading it back*). Patriarchee.

ALEX. Key. Patriar-key.

He adds a note to his book.

SIMON. Patriarkey.

Beat.

And what is –

ALEX. The system in society where men have all the power.

SIMON *writes it down.*

You know you can't go round telling women what to do all the time. We don't like it. It fucks us off.

SIMON. Alex...

ALEX. That's what I mean. That is exactly what I mean. Trying to silence me. Take away my voice.

SIMON. I do not think anybody could silence you.

Beat.

ALEX. You can be really annoying sometimes.

Beat. SIMON *dips his finger in her bowl and flicks milk in her face. She wipes her face and, ignoring him, takes a mouthful of her cereal. Beat. She turns round and sprays it in his face. She laughs. He grabs her. Pushes her over on the sofa. She squeals and shrieks. He gets a cushion puts it over her head and sits on it. He takes her bowl of cereal and starts eating it. He reaches for the remote control and puts the television on.* ALEX *pushes him off, takes her cereal back.*

You're such a twat.

She grabs the remote control and changes it to a music channel.

Music. Kanye West's 'Gold Digger' comes on.

SIMON. Tune, yes?

ALEX (*nods*). Tune.

She turns it right up. They sing along and dance while sitting on the sofa, getting more and more into it. SIMON *gets up and dances on the sofa.* ALEX *laughs. He pulls her up. They dance together, singing along, laughing and giggling, getting sillier and sillier.* JOSEPH *walks back in and turns the music off. They stop dancing. Beat.*

JOSEPH. Remember to sign for those prints.

Beat.

And can one of you empty the fucking dishwasher for once.

He slams the door. SIMON *and* ALEX *look at each other. Beat. They burst out laughing.*

Scene Twelve

JOSEPH *is lying on the floor with his feet up against the wall. Bottle of whisky and a joint. Door slams.*

ALEX *(off and laughing).* You're such an idiot. She hardly even looked at you.

SIMON *(off and laughing).* No, she was looking right at me. Her eyes said she liked me.

ALEX *(off and laughing).* No way. You're just some lanky African to her.

SIMON *(off).* What does lanky mean?

ALEX *(off).* Very handsome.

SIMON *(off).* I do not think you are telling me the whole truth.

ALEX *(off).* I am.

SIMON *(off).* Perhaps you are insulting me?

ALEX *(off).* No.

SIMON *(off).* I think you might be.

ALEX *(off).* Ow, that hurts.

SIMON *(off).* Tell me what the lanky means.

ALEX *(off, laughing).* I told you. Ow.

There is a scuffle outside. ALEX *flings open the door, runs in and jumps over the sofa, followed by* SIMON, *who chases her round, dropping his wallet in the process. He grabs her and puts her in a headlock.*

(Laughing.) Get off me. Don't –

He pulls her onto the floor and tickles her. She screams.

(Laughing.) Get off. *(Pushing him off.)* Get off me, you lanky African.

She kicks him and runs out laughing. He chases her out and up the stairs.

JOSEPH *lies with his whisky and joint. He stares into space.*

Pause. He gets up and picks up SIMON*'s wallet. He sits down in his chair. He looks at it. He opens it. He takes everything out of it and lays it out on the side of his chair. He looks at the money in it, not much; the Oyster card, he unfolds a piece of paper in it. He turns on the light. It is a copy of the photograph, folded up. He looks at it. He puts the money back in the wallet and folds the photograph up and puts it on the table beside him.* SIMON *enters.*

SIMON. I did not know that you were home.

JOSEPH. I am.

SIMON. I thought you were –

JOSEPH. Out. I know.

   Beat.

SIMON. I was looking for my… (*Sees the wallet.*)

   Pause. He moves towards JOSEPH *to take it.* JOSEPH *picks it up and holds it. He holds it out to* SIMON. SIMON *goes to get it and* JOSEPH *holds it away. Cat and mouse.* JOSEPH *puts it on the armchair and* SIMON *gently takes it.* SIMON *sees the folded-up picture. He looks at* JOSEPH. *Pause. He carefully takes it and puts it back in his wallet.*

JOSEPH. I'm trying to figure out why you carry that around with you.

   Beat.

SIMON. I printed it from the computer.

JOSEPH. I can see that.

SIMON. Do you mind?

JOSEPH. Why would I mind?

SIMON. It uses much ink, to print it, it –

JOSEPH. That's the least of my worries.

   Beat.

SIMON. Perhaps you feel…

JOSEPH. Feel what?

SIMON. I wanted to have my own copy.

JOSEPH. Why would you want a copy of that?

Beat.

SIMON. It is the only photograph I have of them.

JOSEPH. Bit weird, carrying round a photo of your murdered
family.

SIMON. Goodnight, Joseph.

He goes to leave.

JOSEPH. If you hurt her.

SIMON *stops.*

She's fragile. She doesn't seem it, but… she needs –

Beat.

She's all I've got.

Beat.

She's all I've got left.

SIMON. This is not true.

JOSEPH. Isn't it?

SIMON. No.

Beat.

You have your photographs.

Scene Thirteen

ALEX *is pacing up and down. The door slams.*

ALEX. Dad?

> SIMON *enters with a pile of paperwork and bag with 'City and Islington College' written on it.*

SIMON. Yes, daughter.

ALEX. Dad was supposed to have a meeting with Paul and Greta yesterday and he didn't turn up. Did you hear him come in last night?

SIMON. No, where is he?

ALEX. I don't know. That's what I'm saying. He's missing.

SIMON. I am sure he is not in any harm.

ALEX. He didn't ring or anything. He –

SIMON. He is not a child. He can take care of himself.

ALEX. But what if something –

SIMON. He is an adult man. He can –

ALEX. But he didn't –

> *The front door opens and slams. The living-room door opens.* JOSEPH *stands, pissed, bedraggled, with a chicken under his arm. They stare at him. He sits down in his chair. They stare at him.*

JOSEPH. What have I missed?

> *Beat.*

Nothing important then.

ALEX. Paul called.

JOSEPH (*to the chicken*). Did you hear that, Mabel?

ALEX. You missed a meeting yesterday.

JOSEPH (*to chicken*). Mabel, we missed a meeting. (*To* ALEX.) Was it important?

ALEX. Yes.

JOSEPH. Mabel, we missed an important meeting. (*Pretends to listen to the chicken.*) Mabel wants to know who was at the meeting.

ALEX. I don't know. It was your meeting.

JOSEPH. My daughter says she doesn't know, which is amazing, because my daughter usually knows everything there is to know about everything in the world.

ALEX *looks at* SIMON.

SIMON. Would you like a glass of water, Joseph? I shall get you a –

JOSEPH (*stands up*). And, Mabel, dear sweet Mabel, this is Simon, the one I was telling you about. (*Leans into the chicken and listens to the response.*) I know, he does, doesn't he?

Beat.

ALEX. Where've you been?

JOSEPH. What's it got to do with you?

ALEX. You've been out all night.

JOSEPH. So?

ALEX. You're a mess.

JOSEPH. So?

ALEX. You stink.

JOSEPH. So?

ALEX. You're talking to a chicken.

JOSEPH. She's got a name, you know.

ALEX. Where've you been?

Beat.

We were worried.

Beat.

What have you been doing?

JOSEPH. I've been doing Jackie.

Beat.

At number ten. We drank some very nice wine, snorted some good coke and then we fucked about three times, courtesy of Jeff's Viagra, that's Jackie's husband, and then we got stoned courtesy of Jackie's son's skunk. Can't remember his name. Jasper or Casper or Wasper or something fucking annoying. Jackie had to leave to pick Jeff up from the airport cos he's been on a golfing holiday to the Dominican Republic with his boring middle-aged fat banking buddies. She told me to help myself to whatever I wanted before I left, so I did. (*Indicates the chicken and pulls out a pair of knickers from his top pocket.*)

Beat.

Is there anything else you and your brother would like to know? I can tell you all about Jackie's vaginal rejuvenation surgery if you like. I'm sure she wouldn't mind, she was quite evangelical about it, I'm sure she –

ALEX. You should go to bed.

JOSEPH. I've been in bed. With Jackie. Haven't you been listening? Although we did fuck in the kitchen as well, on the butcher's block, which was surprisingly nice actually –

ALEX. Thanks but I think we can do without the detail.

JOSEPH. Is it all a bit TMI for you, Alex?

ALEX. Simon, take that thing back to number ten, will you?

SIMON *takes the chicken from* JOSEPH.

SIMON. What shall I –

ALEX. Chuck it over the gate into the garden.

SIMON *goes.*

JOSEPH (*calls*). Bye, Mabel. Better call Paul. (*Looks for the house phone.*) Where is that bastard phone? Why can I never find the fucking phone? (*Looks for it, finds it.*) Gotcha, you little wanker. (*To* ALEX.) Aren't you going to try to stop me?

ALEX. Why would I?

JOSEPH. Because I'm fucked out of my rotten mind.

ALEX. I'm not your babysitter.

He looks at her and dials.

And I'm not Mum.

JOSEPH *throws the phone in the air. It drops on the floor.*

Very grown up.

He laughs and grabs the plastic bag from the floor, empties everything on the floor and puts the bag over his head, pulls it up.

JOSEPH. Ku Klux Klan – best shot of '76.

Pulls it down. Pulls it up.

Guantanamo Bay – runner-up in World Press Awards 2002. Joseph Potter, the most gifted photojournalist of his generation, no situation too horrific, gross, dirty, wretched or pitiful, he'll be there. He'll find it. Or if he doesn't, it will certainly find him.

Pulls it down. Pulls it up.

Lady Gaga.

He starts to sing 'Born This Way' by Lady Gaga.

He sits with the bag on his head, breathing in and breathing out. ALEX *pulls it off his head. She puts the stuff on the floor back into the bag.*

Pause.

Does he wear something?

Beat.

Does he wear a johnny?

Beat.

Does Simon wear a Durex, a love-glove, a cock-sock, whatever you want to call it?

ALEX. What?

JOSEPH. Does he?

ALEX. I have no idea what you're going on about.

JOSEPH. Are you making him cover his prick when he fucks you?

Beat.

ALEX. Oh my God.

JOSEPH. The outcome will not be pretty.

ALEX. Is that what you think?

JOSEPH. Your baby will be a spastic.

ALEX. You're embarrassing yourself, Dad.

JOSEPH. Your baby will be a spastic hunchback hermaphrodite African albino.

ALEX. You're pissed and you're totally out of order –

JOSEPH. It's against the law, you know that, though, don't you?

ALEX. How can you possibly think that we –

JOSEPH. Working in a supermarket and fucking your brother. I've never been so proud.

ALEX. I'm not listening to this.

JOSEPH. You know why it's illegal, I presume, because A – it's morally repulsive, and B – your baby will be a lump of fucking gristle.

ALEX. When you're sober, you'll be –

JOSEPH. I've seen you. The way you look at each other. Like no one is there. Like no one else fucking exists.

Beat.

He's probably got AIDS.

Beat.

He's probably fucked AIDS into you.

SIMON *enters.*

SIMON. The bird is dead.

They look at him.

I threw it over. There was a dog in the garden.

JOSEPH *bursts out laughing.* SIMON *starts laughing with him.* ALEX *stares at them.*

ALEX. Joseph says you've got AIDS.

Beat. SIMON *stops laughing.*

He says you've fucked AIDS into me.

JOSEPH. I said probably. Don't make it sound worse than it was. (*Getting up.*) I'm off to Bedfordshire. Don't wake me.

SIMON. Why do you say this?

JOSEPH. It's a saying from… I don't know where…

SIMON. About the AIDS?

JOSEPH. Because you're fucking my daughter. I mean, your sister.

SIMON. This is not… I am not… We are not… That is –

JOSEPH. Now, if you'll excuse me –

He gets up to go.

SIMON. Stay where you are.

ALEX. Simon…

SIMON. No, he must apologise. To say such a thing as this. He must –

ALEX. Leave it. There's no point –

SIMON. Apologise. How can you say this?

JOSEPH *turns and looks at him.* JOSEPH *laughs.*

It is terrible. Apologise. Now.

SIMON *moves towards him.* ALEX *pulls him back. Beat.*

(*To* ALEX.) I sent Joseph an email four years ago.

JOSEPH *stops*. ALEX *turns to* SIMON.

I emailed him four years ago to say I was looking for you. To say I thought you were my sister. He did not tell you. He has known about me for four years.

Beat.

He kept me away from you.

Beat.

He wanted to keep me away from you.

JOSEPH. Goodnight, one and all.

SIMON. It is the truth.

ALEX (*to* JOSEPH). Don't you dare. Don't you fucking dare leave this room.

He goes.

Scene Fourteen

JOSEPH *sits in another chair drinking coffee and smoking.*
ALEX *sits down on the sofa next to* SIMON, *eating a sandwich, wearing a Sainsbury's uniform.*

ALEX. How's it going?

SIMON. It is complete. Look.

He hands her the form and she reads through it. SIMON *and* JOSEPH *sit in silence.*

ALEX (*to* JOSEPH). Have you written the cheque?

JOSEPH *shakes his head.*

I'll pay you back. Once I get paid. As soon as I get paid.

JOSEPH. Haven't got any cheques left. Ran out.

ALEX. For God's sake.

JOSEPH. I haven't written a cheque for years.

ALEX. They must have sent you another chequebook.

JOSEPH. I told them not to bother.

ALEX. He needs to send it to the Border Agency today.

JOSEPH. No one writes cheques any more. It's like making jokes about Škodas. No one does it.

ALEX. How's he's supposed to –

JOSEPH. How do you double the price of a Škoda?

Beat.

Fill up the tank.

ALEX (*tuts*). I'll write the cheque and you can transfer the money online to my account so I don't go overdrawn and when I'm paid I'll transfer it back.

Beat.

No idea where my chequebook is though…

She gets up and goes out. SIMON *reads over the application form. Silence.*

JOSEPH. How much do you want?

SIMON. The visa extension is five hundred and sixty-one pounds.

JOSEPH. To go home. How much do you want to go home?

Beat.

If you go back, I'll give you what you want.

SIMON *looks at him.*

I've got twenty grand in my current account. You can have it. I can get it today. We can book your flight today.

Beat.

I don't know what you're still doing here.

SIMON. When you sleep, what do you dream?

JOSEPH *closes his eyes.*

JOSEPH. What do you want?

SIMON. I hear you, shouting in the night. What are you –

JOSEPH. With twenty grand, you could buy your own house, some land, get yourself a wife, have some kids. Don't you want that? Isn't that what you want?

SIMON. I am sorry.

JOSEPH. That's no good to me.

JOSEPH looks at him.

If you stay, I will make this impossible for you. I will –

Beat.

You can't come here and –

SIMON. I am sorry that you are the man that you are.

ALEX enters with a chequebook.

ALEX. I found yours, you bloody liar. It was in that drawer with all the keys.

She gives it to JOSEPH. *He looks at the chequebook. Beat. He writes out the cheque and hands it to* SIMON. SIMON *puts the form in an envelope and adds the cheque. He puts it into his bag. He gets up.*

Do you need a stamp?

SIMON (*putting on his coat*). I will buy one from the Post Office.

ALEX (*gets up*). It's okay, I've got some in my bag, I'll just –

SIMON. No, no. Sit. Have your lunch.

He waves her to sit down.

ALEX (*sitting*). Okay, see you later.

He smiles, waves and leaves. The front door closes. ALEX *gets up.*

JOSEPH. Alex.

ALEX. No.

JOSEPH. Just listen.

ALEX. No.

JOSEPH. At some point, you've got to let me explain, you've
    got to –

ALEX. No.

JOSEPH. Why won't you let me –

ALEX. There's nothing you can say.

JOSEPH. It wasn't malicious. It wasn't –

He gets up and holds on to her arm.

I can never get you on your own. I just want to explain.

Beat.

Please, let me. Please.

Beat. She turns to him. Pause.

I got the first email just after Meg's diagnosis.

ALEX. So?

JOSEPH. She was dying. My wife was dying.

ALEX. She wasn't just your wife.

JOSEPH. I know. It was tough for both of us.

ALEX. Don't try and use that as an excuse.

JOSEPH. I'm not, I'm –

ALEX. You weren't even here half the time.

JOSEPH. Come on, that's not –

ALEX. You left me to deal with her, remember?

JOSEPH. Alex...

ALEX. You flew off to some war zone in the arsehole of
    nowhere.

JOSEPH. I had to go to –

ALEX. Off you went whenever you felt like it.

JOSEPH. Stop it.

ALEX. For months at a time, leaving her, leaving us.

JOSEPH. It was my job. I had to –

ALEX. And as soon as she was gone, as soon as she wasn't around any more to pick up the pieces, you retired, because you couldn't cope, because –

JOSEPH. That's not fair.

ALEX. You left Simon to die and then you edited him out, cropped him like one of your fucking pictures. That's not fucking fair.

JOSEPH. That's not how it was.

ALEX. He was trying to find me. My brother. My blood. He was alive and you knew. For four years, you –

JOSEPH. I was going to –

ALEX. You were silent.

JOSEPH. I –

ALEX. For four years, you were silent.

JOSEPH. I –

ALEX. You were silent.

Scene Fifteen

ALEX *and* JOSEPH *are sitting. Evening. He's looking through some paperwork to do with the exhibition.*

ALEX. Are you sure?

JOSEPH. Yep.

ALEX. Are you absolutely –

JOSEPH. I said so, didn't I? It's entirely up to you.

ALEX. Yeah.

JOSEPH. It's your decision.

Beat.

ALEX. I can't believe you're being so cool about it.

JOSEPH. You know me, as cool as Kate Moss, as cool as a Mint Magnum.

ALEX. Yeah, but don't you –

JOSEPH. It's cool.

ALEX. Okay.

Beat.

JOSEPH. The head of the company doing all the PR for the exhibition is called Anita Dick.

ALEX. Bit unfortunate.

JOSEPH. Anita Dick.

ALEX. Yeah, I get it. Her surname's Dick.

JOSEPH. No. Anita Dick – I need a dick. Anita Dick. Anita Dick.

ALEX. Ah.

JOSEPH. I need a dick. That's funny, right?

ALEX. It doesn't really sound like that, though. It sounds like Anita Dick.

JOSEPH. If you say the T like a D then it sounds like I need a dick. I need a dick.

ALEX. Yeah, but it's not a D it's a T. Anita. And it starts with A not I.

JOSEPH. Why are you taking her side?

ALEX. I'm not, I'm just proffering –

JOSEPH. She could do with changing her name. Imagine being born Anita Dick. Poor cow. You should forward her the information.

ALEX. Dad…

JOSEPH. 'What's in a name? That which we call a rose
By any other name would smell as sweet.'

ALEX. Let's talk about it properly, let's –

JOSEPH. No, I'm cool… cool as… Kate… Middleton… no,
not –

ALEX. It's a big deal. I understand that.

JOSEPH. Meg had a friend who changed his name from Ian to
Barcode. He was an anarchist from Whitechapel. He came
round for dinner once and he puked in the kitchen sink on
top of the dirty dishes and didn't even mention it. Meg only
noticed when she went to do the washing up and there was
risotto puke all over Le Creuset. He hadn't said a word.

Beat.

Do you know you're not allowed to change your name to
Bin Laden? It's deemed offensive, they won't let you, the
Deed Poll people. Fucking fascists.

Beat.

How much does it cost to change one's name these days?

ALEX. Thirteen pounds.

JOSEPH. Wow.

Beat.

Thirteen pounds…

Beat.

Two packets of fags. Proper fags. Malboro not Superkings.

ALEX (*getting up*). When you're ready to talk about this
properly, I'll be –

JOSEPH. I'm ready.

ALEX *sits back down. Pause.*

Thirteen pounds…

She gets up.

Meg wanted to call you Edith.

ALEX. I know.

JOSEPH. She made me listen to 'Je ne regrette rien' and when I said Piaf sounded like a goat, she wouldn't speak to me until I apologised.

ALEX. I know.

JOSEPH. Edith. I couldn't have that. They would have crucified you at school. I said that to Meg. And she said we could send you to a Steiner school. Meg knew a kid called Biscuit who went to a Steiner school. Flourished, apparently.

Beat.

Is it his idea?

ALEX. No.

Beat.

It feels like the right thing to do.

JOSEPH *snorts.*

Feels like me.

Beat.

JOSEPH. Frances Mutesi. Miss Mutesi. Miss Frances Mutesi.

ALEX. Dad...

JOSEPH. I'm not calling you that.

ALEX. That's your choice.

JOSEPH. I will never call you that name. Frances fucking Mutesi.

Scene Sixteen

ALEX *has her hands over her eyes with her back to the door. An old suitcase by her side.* SIMON *is offstage.*

ALEX (*calling*). Are you ready yet?

SIMON (*off*). Yes, yes.

ALEX. Come on then.

She turns round to the door. SIMON *walks in wearing an ill-fitting seventies dinner suit in blue velvet with a fat bow tie. She takes one look at him and bursts out laughing.*

SIMON. I like it.

He walks around the room.

I like this material.

She laughs.

What is this material?

ALEX. Velvet.

SIMON (*taking out his notebook*). Velvet.

ALEX. V–E–L–V–E–T.

SIMON (*writes it in his notebook*). Velvet.

ALEX. You look like Eric Morecambe.

SIMON. Thank you.

ALEX (*laughs*). It's not a compliment. You look terrible.

SIMON. I think it is very glamorous.

ALEX. It's an interview at City and Islington College, not Bond school. What else is there?

SIMON opens the suitcase and pulls out a number of suits. All seventies throwbacks.

No one will wear a suit, you know that, don't you?

SIMON. At university, they told us to wear a suit for all the interviews.

ALEX. Everyone will be casual. They'll all be –

SIMON. I need to be taken seriously.

ALEX looks at him. She starts to take off his bow tie.

ALEX. We'll go shopping tomorrow. We can go to Topman.

SIMON. I do not want the skinny jeans.

ALEX (*laughs*). Alright, no skinny jeans.

He takes the jacket off and the shirt off. JOSEPH walks in with a portfolio under his arm. He stops.

We were just –

SIMON. For my interview.

JOSEPH. With the immigration police?

ALEX. Very funny.

SIMON. I am allowed to apply for the college place. I am allowed –

JOSEPH. For Christ's sake, it was a joke.

He sees the clothes. Beat.

ALEX. They were in the loft.

Beat.

We went up into the loft and…

Beat.

I didn't think you'd mind. I thought…

Beat.

You don't wear them. You haven't worn them for –

JOSEPH (*to SIMON, hands him his keys*). Here –

Beat.

(*Hands him keys.*) You may as well have these. (*Shows him.*) That's for my car, that's the house, but you know that already, because you've got your own set. That's for my bike. It's in the shed. The key for the shed's somewhere here – (*Looks in the drawer.*) Aha, here you go. (*Hands him the keys.*)

ALEX. There's no need for –

JOSEPH (*takes his wallet out*). Let's see what else I've got here. (*Takes out the money and counts it.*) Ten, twenty, thirty, fifty, seventy, ninety pounds – (*Puts the money on the table and digs around in his pocket taking out the change.*) and twenty, thirty, five, six – thirty-six pence. (*Picks up the notes and the change and opens* SIMON*'s hands and puts the money in his hand.*) Ninety pounds and thirty-six pence. There you go.

ALEX. Have you finished?

.JOSEPH (*looking in wallet*). You may as well have my driving licence too. In fact, fuck it, have the whole thing. (*Chucks the wallet at him.*) And while we're at it – (*Takes off his jacket and chucks it on the sofa.*) You can take that, you might not want it, though. (*Unbuttoning his shirt.*) Smells a bit. Just needs a dry-clean, I expect. (*Takes his shirt off.*) This is from Paul Smith. Bloody expensive, but hey, you're worth it.

JOSEPH starts putting the shirt on SIMON*, lifting his arms up and dressing him.* SIMON *stands there.*

You can do the buttons up yourself.

JOSEPH walks away. SIMON *stands still.*

I said you can do the buttons up yourself.

SIMON *stands there.*

Okay, okay, I'll be mother.

He goes over and starts doing the shirt buttons up.

ALEX. Dad.

SIMON *lets him.*

JOSEPH. Yes, dear?

ALEX. Stop it.

JOSEPH. Stop what, dear? There, there, all done now.

He taps SIMON*'s face. He does it again a little harder. And again. And again.* SIMON *grabs hold of his fist. Pause.*

JOSEPH *pulls away. Pause*.

Let's get a Chinese tonight. On me.

Pause.

How about an Indian?

Beat.

Pizza then. That's settled. Pizza it is. Not Domino's though. I fucking hate Domino's.

He starts looking for the phone.

Where's the phone? Why does no one put that fucking phone back? By the way, I've got a meeting in Manchester tomorrow. I'll be gone for a couple of days. When I get back, I want him gone.

ALEX. What?

JOSEPH. I want him gone.

ALEX. Where do you expect him to go?

JOSEPH. Sweden, Berwick-upon-Tweed, machete land. I don't care.

ALEX. You can't –

JOSEPH. It's time he left.

ALEX. But –

JOSEPH. I want him fucking gone.

Beat.

It's making me sick.

Beat.

Looking at him every day is making me –

SIMON. I am not leaving.

ALEX (*to* SIMON). Shsh.

JOSEPH. Get out.

ALEX. No, Dad, it's –

JOSEPH. Get your stuff and get the fuck away from us.

Beat.

I'm going to count to ten and then I swear –

ALEX. Stop it.

SIMON. Then what?

Beat.

What will you do?

Beat.

Joseph?

Beat.

What will happen next in this story?

Pause.

That is what I thought.

Silence.

Tell her.

Beat.

Tell her.

ALEX. Tell me what?

Beat.

SIMON. The reason Joseph left me in Rwanda.

ALEX. I know the reason.

SIMON. He could not carry us both.

ALEX. Yeah.

SIMON *laughs.*

There wasn't time.

SIMON *laughs.*

(*To* JOSEPH.) There wasn't, was there, Dad?

JOSEPH. The Interahamwe were coming –

ALEX. I know.

SIMON. Tell her.

JOSEPH. It was chaos, a living hell.

ALEX. I know.

SIMON. The reason you left me behind.

JOSEPH. It was the worst thing, I've ever seen. It was the worst thing, I'd ever been involved in. I was –

SIMON. Busy.

Beat.

He was busy.

ALEX. What?

SIMON. He was arranging our mother.

Beat.

Into a pretty picture.

Beat.

He came into the church. He saw the bodies. He walked around taking his pictures. He saw our mother and you asleep by her side. He picked you up and he moved you from her. He waited for you to begin to cry. He took our mother's hand and pulled it out, like this – (*Unfurls hand.*) and he waited. He watched you crawl towards her body and when your hand reached hers, he took his photograph.

Silence.

JOSEPH. Alex, I –

ALEX. I'm starving.

Beat.

Who wants pizza?

Silence. She goes to the drawer and gets a pile of takeaway flyers.

Anybody?

Pause.

(*Selecting the Domino's.*) Just me then.

Beat.

(*Looking at flyer.*) I think the medium Meatilicious should do it.

Beat.

Or maybe a Quattro Formaggi.

JOSEPH. You've got to understand –

ALEX. I'm not sharing by the way.

JOSEPH. The pressure that I was –

ALEX. You can both fuck off if you think I'm sharing.

Beat.

JOSEPH. There was no time to –

ALEX. Because you wasted it.

JOSEPH. I wanted –

ALEX. Because you waited.

JOSEPH. That's not –

ALEX. Because you wanted to see me suffer.

JOSEPH. You don't understand.

ALEX. You constructed it.

JOSEPH. Please try to understand.

ALEX. It's made up. I understand.

Pause.

JOSEPH. The essence of the shot is true.

Pause.

It was horrific, the slaughter, the blood, the machetes…

Beat.

You'd lost your mother, your father, you'd witnessed…

Beat.

The grief is true.

ALEX. The grief? It's my grief. Mine.

JOSEPH. I know, darling, I know it –

ALEX. Wasn't a church full of slaughtered villagers enough for you?

JOSEPH. I wanted people to take notice of it. I thought if I could just –

ALEX. Squeeze some tears out of the little black baby –

JOSEPH. I thought it –

ALEX. For the good white folk back home.

JOSEPH. It was to stop it. I took it to stop the –

ALEX. And did it stop?

Beat.

JOSEPH. Look, I did what I thought was best.

ALEX. Right.

JOSEPH. The world had to know what was –

ALEX. Why? What did knowing do?

Beat.

What does knowing actually do?

JOSEPH. Alex, come on now, it's –

ALEX. Knowing does fuck all.

JOSEPH. Listen, I've given my life to –

ALEX. Yeah.

JOSEPH. I've seen the worst side of humanity –

ALEX. Yeah.

JOSEPH. And ruined any hope of peace in my own mind so –

ALEX. Ne regrette rien, Joseph, ne regrette rien.

JOSEPH. Don't you dare. Don't you fucking dare –

ALEX. And what did you do when you saw the worst side of humanity?

Beat.

You took pictures.

JOSEPH. I bore witness.

ALEX. You took pictures.

Beat.

JOSEPH. And I saved you.

ALEX. Yeah, the little black wretch rescued by the big white hero, your symbol of hope in a rotten world, showing me off like a fucking trophy.

JOSEPH. Like a daughter.

ALEX. Someone else's daughter –

JOSEPH. We loved you –

ALEX. That you stole to give your barren wife as a playmate while you roamed the world, feeding off misery.

JOSEPH. Alex…

ALEX. Stop calling me that.

JOSEPH. We loved you with all our –

ALEX. You went to the other side of the world when your wife was dying. You left her. For what? A photograph.

Beat.

You've stood by and watched people tortured, murdered, starved to death. For what? A photograph.

Beat.

(*Pointing at* SIMON.) You left him to be killed. For what?

Pause.

SIMON. Joseph wanted me dead.

JOSEPH. No, I –

SIMON. He saw me watching him when he took his photograph.

JOSEPH. No.

SIMON. It is the truth.

JOSEPH. I didn't. I saw you after. When I was leaving, I –

SIMON. You saw me watching you. That is why you did not take me as well.

Beat.

ALEX. You left him because he saw what you did...

JOSEPH. No, I told you, I couldn't carry you both. The Interahamwe were coming.

SIMON. The Interahamwe did not come back.

JOSEPH. Yes, I heard them. They were –

SIMON. No. You know they did not come back.

Beat.

ALEX. You left him because you were afraid that he'd tell someone...

JOSEPH. No.

ALEX. Yes.

SIMON. No.

Beat.

He left me because when he looked at me, in the church, into my eyes, he saw the man he truly is.

Beat.

Joseph left me to die, because he saw the truth and it was unbearable for him.

Scene Seventeen

ALEX *stands with her bags packed. She stands and looks at*
JOSEPH. *He stands and looks at her.*

JOSEPH. I can give you a lift.

ALEX. It's alright, a cab's on its way.

JOSEPH. I can take you –

ALEX. It's fine. A cab's fine.

JOSEPH. It's no problem. I'll just –

ALEX. You won't be able to get back in time for the opening do.

JOSEPH. That doesn't matter.

ALEX. Paul will be expecting you. They'll all be expecting
you.

JOSEPH. It doesn't matter. I'll get my car keys.

ALEX. No… really. No.

Pause.

JOSEPH. Have you got everything?

ALEX. Yep.

JOSEPH. Well, I can send you anything. Whatever you've
forgotten. Whatever you need.

ALEX. Thanks.

Pause.

JOSEPH. Will you phone when you get there? To let me know
that you've arrived. Just to, you know, to let me know.

Beat.

Have you got something to read?

ALEX. I've downloaded *Mad Men*.

JOSEPH. It's supposed to be very good. *Mad Men*. You'll enjoy
that.

ALEX. Yeah.

JOSEPH. One of those things that passed me by. Like *The Wire*. Never saw that either. Too late now. Have you seen *The Wire*?

ALEX. Yeah.

JOSEPH. Good?

ALEX. Yeah.

JOSEPH. And *The Killing*. Everyone's always going on about *The Killing*. The window cleaner said he'd lend me his box set next time he does his round. He's got *Borgen* as well. Got it off his brother-in-law.

Pause.

You know you can always come back.

ALEX. Yeah.

JOSEPH. I mean it. You're always welcome.

ALEX. Yeah.

JOSEPH. I'll keep your room. For when you do, for when you come back.

Pause.

Have you got some food? Something to eat for the journey.

ALEX. I don't need –

JOSEPH. There are some boiled eggs in the fridge. Jackie gave me some of her eggs. Well, not her eggs, some of her chicken's eggs. They've been overlaying, whatever that means. I could make you an egg-mayonnaise sandwich. We've got some capers. I could put capers in it. You used to love that. I could make you that right now. Shall I? Shall I do that?

ALEX. There'll be food on the plane.

SIMON *enters with bags. Pause.* ALEX*'s mobile rings. She answers.*

Yep, we'll be out in a moment, thanks. Thanks.

SIMON *steps forward to shake* JOSEPH*'s hand.*

SIMON. Goodbye, Joseph.

A moment. JOSEPH *shakes it.* SIMON *goes.* ALEX *picks up her bag.* ALEX *and* JOSEPH *look at each other.*

JOSEPH. Have you got enough money?

ALEX. Yes.

JOSEPH. Are you sure? (*Getting out his wallet.*) Because I can give you –

ALEX. There's no need.

JOSEPH. If you need anything, anything at all, just call me. Will you? Will you do that for me?

Pause.

ALEX. Good luck with the exhibition, Dad.

Beat.

JOSEPH. Thank you.

Beat.

Thank you.

The End.

A Nick Hern Book

The Witness first published in Great Britain in 2012 as a paperback original by Nick Hern Books Limited, 14 Larden Road, London W3 7ST, in association with the Royal Court Theatre, London

The Witness copyright © 2012 Vivienne Franzmann

Vivienne Franzmann has asserted her right to be identified as the author of this work

Cover image: feastcreative.com
Cover design: Ned Hoste

Typeset by Nick Hern Books, London
Printed in the UK by Mimeo Ltd, Huntingdon, Cambridgeshire PE29 6XX

A CIP catalogue record for this book is available from the British Library

ISBN 978 1 84842 250 6